LITURGICAL DANCE

A Practical Guide to Dancing in Worship

By Deena Bess Sherman, M.A.

Printed in the United States of America

Library of Congress Catalog Card Number: 2004105387

ISBN: 0-7880-2123-0

For Kyra, Lanie, and Alex, who always remind me to dance. Their dancing has brought me more joy than anything else in my life.

Special thanks to:

David E. Mertz, my husband, who brought a deep sense of joy and peace into my life, which enabled me to finally finish this project! He's my best proofreader, best critic, computer geek, and best friend.

Darla Sherman Christensen, my sister, who encouraged me to speak freely. She inspired and motivated me from conception to completion of this project.

My mother, Kira Karsten Woodruff, who took me to church and to dance classes from as far back as I can remember. She introduced me to God and she introduced me to dance. How do you thank someone for that?!

Daniel W. Borchers, my ex-husband, who encouraged dance in all the parishes we served over nearly two decades. His opinions and proofreading skills were invaluable.

My friend, Indi Dieckgrafe, Associate Professor of Dance at Saint Mary's College in Notre Dame, Indiana, who checked my French.

CONTENTS

Preface

This piece of writing is an odd hybrid of scholarly paper, personal testimony, and practical guide concerning liturgical dance. It began when I was in seminary and did an independent study on dance. Part of it ended up in an article, published in the professional journal, *Currents in Theology and Mission* in 1991. The long version sat in a file, which I would sometimes pull out and think about expanding. I would smile at the computerless typing and rich cotton paper of a time not so long ago, and inevitably a baby would cry for me and I'd put it away for another year.

Many years passed. I continued to dance. With each new dance I had new insights about dance in the Christian Church. I thought again how I should pull out that paper and type it into a full length book which would include the history, my experience, and some practical choreography for newcomers to the dance. Finally I decided that if I did not do it in 2004, I never would.

My purpose here is not to be absolutely comprehensive, but rather to be practical. I want to give the reader, who wishes to dance in his or her church, the tools to get started. I want to share the ways dance has touched my life and molded my relationship with God. I want to share the things I learned about leading groups of dancers in Christian Churches.

This book is very obviously from the perspective of a seminary-trained Lutheran and a classical ballet-trained dancer. I understand that there are many other perspectives on both sacred dance and theology. This is mine.

Some minor things you will notice: dates are in C.E. (Common Era) rather than A.D. (Anno Domini). When scripture is quoted, it is the New Revised Standard Version, unless otherwise noted. I have included my references within the text rather than using footnotes or endnotes.

You will see the words church (small c) and Church (proper noun). The former is a general term, referring to buildings, the second is used when I refer to the Christian movement as a whole, not confined to any particular branch of it, though most of my observations happen to be about the Western Church. As some of you know, the Church split in 1054 into Eastern (Orthodox) and Western (Roman Catholic). The Western Church begat Lutheranism. My experience with the Eastern Church is limited.

I have tried to be helpful and brief, giving the most possible information about this subject, in the smallest space. If there are things you feel should be included when I update this, please feel free to contact me at deenabess@yahoo.com.

God bless your dancing!

Deena

Dancing for my husband's installation as pastor of
Grace Lutheran Church in Aurora, Illinois in 1995
Photo by Ray Trembacki

Chapter 1
What Is Liturgical Dance?

Dance has been a part of human spirituality since humans have sought the divine. It crosses lines of time, geography, and culture. From Shiva (Hindu), who danced the world into being and through the dance holds it in sacred order, to the Shakers (Christian sect), who danced to receive the gift of prophecy, dance appears in some form within most human expressions of spirituality. Like laughter, compassion, or awareness of consciousness, the impulse toward expressive movement is simply one of the attributes of our humanness. It has been one of the primary ways we have reached for transcendence throughout the ages. As Thomas Kane writes, "Dance, the most universal of all the arts, is movement ordered by rhythm, time, and space, expressing life and its deepest mysteries. Before speech, dance was the medium of communication of the human to the divine." (Kane, p.93)

It is not my purpose here to showcase the many ways dance has been utilized in other religious traditions, though we need not look very far to see it. A Native American Pow Wow or display of Jewish folk dancing will remind us of the esteem in which dance is generally held within spiritual gatherings. If you are looking for a wider picture of dance as a universal spiritual art, I recommend Iris J. Stewart's book, *Sacred Woman, Sacred Dance*.

The questions before us as Christian dancers and worship leaders who wish to add dance to our worship, include: "was dance ever a part of the Christian tradition?" and "can dance be used TODAY in the Christian worship of which I am a part." I can answer the first question with a resounding YES! The second question, you must answer for yourself and I will attempt in this book, to help you do that. If dance is indeed something you believe would bring blessings to your worshipping community, this book includes concrete suggestions for getting started. I have included choreography for six dances, with music for four of them. This book is intended as a starting point and guide for bringing dance into your Christian worship.

Dance has been a part of Christian worship since there has been Christian worship. Indeed it is older than our formal creeds and our hymns. It is older than written liturgy or even standardized prayers. When Christians began to worship, they expressed themselves with the words and movements God's Spirit gave them. Whether the converts to Christianity were from Judaism or other religions of the region at that time, dance was one of the ways in which their spirituality was likely expressed. It was natural for people to wish to bring dance, then, into Christian worship. We will look more closely at this in the next chapter.

What is "liturgical?"

The word "liturgical" denotes something which pertains to the act of worship. A liturgy is an agreed upon formula for people to use as they worship together. Most Christian groups have a liturgy or set of liturgies written down for use in all churches of their sect or denomination. A Roman Catholic or Methodist or Lutheran can walk into most any church in America of that particular denomination and know the worship will follow the same basic form. They can depend on the order of the elements in worship and the language to be familiar to them. Indeed the words spoken between the worship leader and congregation will be precisely the same from one congregation to another within a denomination if they utilize the same hymnal, with the same order of worship. This is having a common liturgy. Thus, when we speak of "liturgical churches" we are speaking of those with a common formula for how a worship service should be conducted.

As a life long member of the Lutheran Church, I am most familiar with their liturgical forms, so I will use them as an example. Lutheran liturgy was originally written by Martin Luther and was based on the Roman Catholic

Mass. It maintains elements with lovely Latin names, like: the agnus dei (lamb of God), the gloria patri (glory to the father), and the nunc diminis (now dismiss). These elements often involve verbal or sung interaction between the worship leader and congregants. Each of the elements has a place and a meaning, all of which builds to the climax of the worship experience, the eucharist (holy communion), where we meet God in the tangible elements of bread and wine.

Lutherans, like Roman Catholics and others, are very proud of their liturgies and feel that these help them to worship God in a beautiful and respectful form. Though many Lutheran congregations are now offering worship which does not use their traditional liturgies, the worship services still follow a similar order of worship. They utilize many of the same elements, though with different words and a wider variety of media.

Liturgy can be a two-edged sword. While the beautiful, timeless words and melodies can be burned into one's consciousness and enhance joy when one feels joy or bring comfort when one feels the whole world is coming apart, familiarity can also breed complacency and insularity.

When I was a child in the Lutheran Church-Missouri Synod, our hymnal was called "The Lutheran Hymnal," referred to as TLH. As a child I had mixed feelings about the archaic language within the beautiful, timeless melodies. I spent a great deal of time as an adolescent in prayer, meditation, and even fasting. I would wake up with pieces of the old liturgy playing in my head. I was excited by Christianity. I wanted to devote my life to it. I wanted to find a way to bring its joy to everyone.

I remember standing in the pews one cold, snowy Sunday in Ellicottville, N.Y. (it seemed like 9 months of the year were cold there). I was singing the Gloria in Excelsis as loudly as propriety would allow, "Glory be to God on high: And on earth peace, good will toward men. We praise Thee, we bless Thee, we worship Thee, we give thanks to Thee, for Thy great glory . . . . "

For some reason, on this day, I took my eyes off the altar and looked around. I saw dozens of older German Lutherans, singing these same words with the stony faces of German stoicism. Looking back I realize that it was that determination and stoicism which had allowed some of them to survive things I could not possibly imagine, but at the time I didn't think about who they were or why their demeanors were so impassive, I simply became confused. How could they experience this so differently than I did? It was all I could do not to jump up and dance! I decided all the excitable folks like myself must be up in the choir loft!

Over the years, I have seen many worship services full of people with, what some pastors call, "the holstein stare." I have also seen liturgy in places where everyone was so passionate about the worship that I was certain the words held the power to move mountains. I understand that people show passion for God differently. So for better or worse, there is a glimpse of "liturgical churches."

"Non-liturgical churches" would then be those with no particularly prescribed order of service, though the order of elements in their services are often the same from week to week and even from congregation to congregation. In many of them we see a pattern of congregational singing (maybe 15-30 minutes), followed by a sermon or bible study, and then, perhaps, an altar call.

What is strikingly different about worship in non-liturgical churches is the lack of spoken, sung, or chanted exchanges between the worship leader and people.

As we will see in the next chapter, dance is one of Christianity's many rich liturgical inheritances from our Jewish roots. It is another form of interaction between worship leader and worshippers, as well as between the worshippers and God.

It has fallen in and out of favor over the centuries and has taken on many forms. Its use or disuse has reflected the changing roles of clergy and laity throughout Christian history. Its beauty, blessing, and pageant have been a testament to the work of God's Holy Spirit inspiring artists through the ages.

Liturgical dance is one facet of sacred dance. In their 1984 book, *Introducing Dance in Christian Worship*, Ronald Gagne, Thomas Kane, and Robert VerEecke define sacred dance as prayer. This is one way to distinguish it from all other forms of dance. Sacred dance falls into three categories: ecstatic movement: imposing a trance or altered state; ritualistic dance: an entire ceremony is danced; and liturgical dance, where it is part of a larger ritual structure (Gagne, p. 95). There have been, and continue to be, Christian groups whose use of dance encompasses all three of these categories. This book will address only liturgical dance.

In defining "liturgical dance" there is a wide range of thought. Some would say that any expressive movement within the context of worship should be considered liturgical dance. This is the viewpoint of Doug Adams in his book, *Congregational Dancing In Christian Worship* (Sharing Company, 1971). This would include kneeling, making the sign of the cross (both by individuals in the congregation and the pastor as he speaks the name of Father, Son and Holy Spirit), bowing one's head or raising one's arms in prayer, and so on.

Others would limit the place of dance to a professional performance art, as we find in Judith Rock's 1988 publication, *Performer as Priest & Prophet*. Many who enjoy liturgical dance would place it somewhere between these poles. I believe it is unhelpful to try and set a strict definition, when it covers a range of spiritual expressions. In this book I will concentrate on one "flavor" of liturgical dance, yet I acknowledge there are many others.

My Dance

In 1985 my ex-husband, Dan, served St. Stephen's Lutheran Church in Wilmington, Delaware as a seminary intern. I had graduated from Valparaiso University just days before our wedding and the cross-country move from Chicago to Wilmington. In an effort to make me feel a part of the congregation, a member of the congregation, named Wendy Betts, asked if I would like to sing in the choir. I respectfully declined, as my thin alto voice is not good for much beyond singing along with the car radio. Wendy then suggested committees, activities, musical performance, and drama. I decided to teach fourth and fifth grade Sunday school, but Wendy was certain that more of my gifts needed to be employed. One day she came to me, barely able to contain herself and said, "you work over at the gymnastics school, right?"

"That's right," I replied warily.

"You've studied a lot of dance?"

"classical ballet, tap, and jazz."

"LITURGICAL DANCE!!" She exploded with glee.

14

"Liturgical dance?" I repeated, trying to envision what these words might mean. I knew liturgical meant that it had to do with worship, but I had never seen or heard of such a thing before. "Is that done?" I asked.

"Of course it is! You'll be wonderful. I'll get some music to you by the end of the week!"

I had no idea that conversation would change my life forever. Indeed, Wendy gave me music and encouragement and on our last Sunday in Wilmington, I danced my own choreography with some of the young women of that parish. The feeling of joy to be able to give something back to that parish who had helped prepare us for our future ministries was thrilling.

As Dan began his final year of seminary in Chicago, I began my first. As I planned my coursework, I deliberately planned to learn more about the history and theology of this thing called liturgical dance. In 1990 I published an article on the subject in a professional journal for clergy, *Currents in Theology and Mission*.

During my years at seminary I danced many times and had the honor to study with and sometimes perform with some young men and women who were both scholars and artists. I choreographed for the Constituting Convention of the Evangelical Lutheran Church in America, when three major Lutheran Church bodies, the LCA, the ALC, and AELC, merged into one. It was stunning to see the UIC Pavilion in Chicago turned into a worship space for 5000 people! I treasure those memories.

Translating dance into parish worship in the years that followed brought a variety of experiences. The unique obstacles and rich rewards of dance in both the parishes our family served and in the parishes of the colleagues I visited over the years, have provided me with insights I could not have imagined when I began. I have danced in store-front churches, large, formal spaces, and everything in between.

Reactions have ranged from enthusiastic praise to one man in Wisconsin telling me, "I could feel the breeze blow by me as you danced past, but I was afraid to look!"

Though he was uncertain about dance in church, I loved the words he chose to express it. In Hebrew the word "ruach" is used for wind, breath, and spirit. God's breath, Holy Spirit, resides in the gentle promptings and fresh breezes that touch us both in worship and in our daily lives. Sometimes we respond and sometimes we are afraid. Sometimes we look and sometimes we simply feel. A dancer should seek to be a vessel for that Spirit. Always.

It is my hope that the things I learned in my research and in those years of choreographing and performing dance in many different circumstances might help to inform others who would add dance to the everyday worship life of congregations across the country.

Your Dance

Congregants in mainline liturgical Christian parishes, who have been exposed to liturgical dance, generally have the expectation that dance is to be performed by people who have a God-given aptitude for it. They do not expect to be asked to dance, and most would refuse, or at least hesitate, if they were asked.

We no longer live in a culture in which dance is a natural part of life for all people. We do not have barn dances, we do not all learn to waltz at an early age as our great grandparents most likely did, and we probably do not polka unless we live in Wisconsin. Dance is not the integral part of our social fabric it once was. Those who did not learn traditional dances a few generations ago, were at a distinct disadvantage. It was expected. Now, not learning to dance is more the norm.

In the absence of common dances being part of our cultural literacy, we look to those who study and practice dance to do the dancing for us in worship. This works in much the same way we look to the choir to sing the more difficult pieces of music within our worship or trained musicians to accompany our songs.

Please keep in mind that I speak here primarily of white Americans of European descent, whose families have resided in this country for multiple generations, and who attend mainline liturgical churches. There are, thankfully, still many cultures, who believe dance is essential to everyday life.

One example is found in the students to whom I taught English for years. They were primarily first generation immigrants from Mexico. They danced. They all could dance. Each semester I invited my class to my home for a fiesta. The dancing was joyous and beautiful.

Understanding the culture(s) and expectations within your worshipping community is essential. A dance which brings great blessing to one group, might be met with wide eyed shock and disgust when used in another venue. I cannot emphasize enough the importance of discerning the needs, styles, and expectations of the worshipping community you serve, when planning and executing liturgical dance!

As I stated earlier, there is a wide range of activity, which can be called liturgical dance. It is the duty of the dancers and worship leaders to discern which of these are worshipful for the people they serve. Never take this responsibility lightly! It is a holy commission to bring dance to worship. When dance is done well, it is a blessing, which, I believe, makes the angels themselves smile. When the wrong dance is presented, it detracts from the worship itself. It is annoying at best, destructive at worst, and may close the door to future dancing in that place.

A few years ago a colleague of mine danced at a church in the city where I live. It was a beautiful dance, masterfully executed, but it did not fit the worship service. She may have been unfamiliar with that congregation and their worship. I came to see her and was struck with how much this seemed like a performance. Though it was a very high quality performance, it did not blend easily into the worship. Many of the congregants were confused. It took me months to win back the trust of the staff at that church so I could reintroduce dance to that place.

I know there have been times when I have also been guilty of thinking first of my dance and only second of the worship as a whole. This is perhaps the most difficult part of liturgical dance--remembering that the overall worship ALWAYS comes first. Dancers and choreographers must always be mindful: *it is not about you!* It is not about what "tricks" you can perform. It is not about what you *want* to do. It is about prayer. It is about where God's Spirit leads you. You are a vessel. You are a humble servant, bringing a gift from God to others. The people who are worshipping don't need to know you, they need to know the God you serve. It is very much like an organist who sits where he or she cannot be seen. The music flows into the worship seamlessly and no one thinks about who is playing it. People did not come to church for an organ concert, they came to worship. It is exactly the same with dance.

I dwell a bit on this topic because this is particularly difficult for trained dancers. Anyone who has studied dance for any length of time and with any degree of seriousness, knows the culture of performance. It is often a petty world of cut-throat competition. Those who are successful professionally are usually the people who thrive best in such an atmosphere, so transferring such talent to a venue with opposite expectations can be daunting! It is essential that anyone who dances understands that the focus must always remain on the communication between God and the worshippers. While the quality of the dancing is very important, this is not primarily a performance of dance. The dance is one of the elements of worship, which facilitates this communication between God and the worshippers. Performance should be done at recitals. Liturgical dance is something very different.

God's Dance

The two best dances I ever did, I did not create. This is as it should be. I have created many dances for God, looking for inspiration, and praying for God's spirit to fill me. In the end, however, they were products of a collaborative effort between me and God's Spirit. On a couple of very special occasions, it was a very different experience.

In 1987 I traveled with the choir from the Lutheran School of Theology at Chicago. At the first stop, I was dancing within a vespers service. My part was very limited. I danced forward with a votive and lit the paschal candle. Then I sat in the sacristy and enjoyed the music of the choir.

After hearing one of the pieces the choir sang--an African piece, which the choir director had brought back with him from a recent visit to Africa--I began dancing where no one could see me. At the next stop, it was a daytime performance and I was to wait outside in the sunlight after doing my processional piece. When they sang the African arrangement, I began to dance again. When they finished, the music continued in my head and I danced and danced. The dance created itself. It screamed to be let out, so I danced it. I danced it alone.

Each time they performed, I danced to that wonderful African piece. I danced it to God because it was a gift that needed to be returned in gratitude. At one stop, some of the members of the tour saw me and suggested I dance it the next time this piece was performed. The director said no. It had not been part of the plan and it would not be added. The choir was so insistent that this dance would add blessings to their performance that he finally relented and let me dance it. I loved that dance. It brought blessings. But I didn't create it. It simply begged to be let out. I have never felt as close to God as I did when I danced this.

The other dance was for a funeral in Brookfield, Illinois. This dance will be discussed in a later chapter. I did arrange this dance. My friend, Eric, a Lutheran pastor, called me one day and said, "I would like you to dance at our church."

I had danced there before, so I said, "OK, when?"

"In two days. It's a funeral. I'm sorry it's short notice, but that's the nature of this sort of thing. I could tell by his voice that he truly cared for these people and it would be a difficult funeral for him to do. "She was a teacher and a dancer," he explained, "and her husband would like dance at her funeral. She was your age. It was a car accident."

I hesitated. I didn't want to do the wrong thing at a funeral where the grief would be as naked as it would be at this one. "Let me think about it," I answered. "I know the music for it, but I'm not sure I can do it."

The hymn "Now the Green Blade Rises" had popped into my head. I had used that for a dance one Easter and suddenly the song was playing loudly in my mind, the words about death and resurrection surfaced out of my memory and I knew it must be right.

A few hours later I agreed. Then I prayed and cried and prayed and planned, and prayed. I wanted to include her students, so I choreographed the dance you will see in chapter 8.

When it came time to dance, I began. I interacted with the other dancers, as planned, and I was told it was lovely. I was rattled to the core, though, when I had absolutely no memory of it. It felt very strange. I remembered standing in the narthex looking at her ballet slippers and pictures of her with her students. I remembered crying and having a very difficult time collecting myself before it was time for the dance to begin. Then I didn't remember anything until I stood next to her husband after the service. I didn't remember doing it. I wasn't even sure I had. It was one of the strangest moments of my life.

The husband of the late dancer greeted me with tears after the service. As his voice cracked, he whispered to me. "I was watching *her* dance. I felt like I was watching Renee (his late wife). Thank you. I felt like she was here." It still makes me shake when I remember that day. I was a vessel.

I am always tempted to take great pride in what I do. But I have learned to know better. It's not about me. It's about God reaching out to his people. It's about me learning to humbly allow God's Spirit to move through me.

It has been my experience that people sense whether I am dancing something because I like that particular piece or whether God is speaking to them and I'm simply a vessel for that holy voice. When it's the latter, it is sometimes exhausting beyond words. The comfort, however, is in knowing that it was right. I don't worry, when that happens, that I "performed" adequately. I don't even ask that question, because I didn't "perform." God spoke.

I wish they were all that way, but they are not. Many are simply things I produce, on a schedule, for a congregation, which expects to see dance every X number of weeks in their worship. That's fine and that is also a blessing, but that is where discernment becomes vital.

While most people in the pews of Christian Churches do not expect to be asked to get up and dance without prior warning, they also do not expect to see dance at a professional level within their worship. When this happens, some congregations are grateful to receive such a rare treat, while others are intimidated--and even offended--by the dissonance they feel professional level performance art brings to their humble, contemplative worship. Conversely, one does not jam a folk dance into the middle of high church liturgy at a formal event, without considering how this fits into the overall context.

I will say it again: **it is vitally important to know the worshipping community before planning dance within their worship**. The dance must be an element of worship, which will complement and enrich the worship as a whole, not sound like a loud note sung off-key in the middle of a song.

For this reason, I will describe dances in this book, which can be performed by many different types of groups, with varying skill levels. It is up to the reader to choose which types of dance will bring a blessing to his or her worshipping community.

Chapter 2
History

This is at the Constituting Convention of the Evangelical Lutheran Church in America,
October 1987.
Photo by Deena Sherman

The history of dance is not the primary focus of this book. There are books which give a more complete history, and if this is of interest to you, I suggest the books by Marilyn Daniels, J.G. Davies, and Ronald Gage, *et al.*, which are listed in the bibliography.

Judaism and Early Christianity

The first Christians were Jews who believed their Messiah had arrived. They lived and worshipped as Jews. What separated them from other Jews was their belief that their messianic prophecies were fulfilled in the person of Jesus of Nazareth. Jews, both then and now, are an expressive people who used dance as a part of their festivals and celebrations. J.F. Davies writes, "The religion

of ancient Israel was without question a dancing one."
(Davies p. 96)

Dance, for Israel was a sacred expression of faith, one
worthy of heaven itself. Daniels writes, "The idea of
heavenly beings encircling the throne of God and singing
his praise goes back to the Talmud, where dancing is
described as being the principle function of the angels."
(Daniels p. 18)

The early Christians saw their following of Jesus as
simply being an extension of Judaism. He was the long-
awaited Messiah of Israel. Their worship, then, was also
an extension of their long tradition. Walter Sorrell tells us,
"The string of dancing prophets continues with Jesus, as
described in the apocryphal Acts of John. The often
violent opposition to dancing by the Church Fathers
throughout the centuries has made us forget the significant
role of dance in the life of the early Christians." (Sorrell p.
19)

So now you're thinking: I know the Acts of the
Apostles and I know the Gospel of John. I even know
about I John, but what is this "Acts of John?"

In the Gospel of John, chapter 20, verse 30, we read,
"Now Jesus did many other signs in the presence of his
disciples, which are not written in this book . . . . " The
Acts of John would be one of those many documents
containing things which Jesus did, "which are not written
in this book" or any other book of the accepted Christian
Bible. The Acts of John, written around the year 120 of the
Common Era, is an apocryphal Gnostic writing. It is one
of the many things written about Jesus' days on earth. It
tells the story Jesus before his arrest and crucifixion,
instructing his followers with both words and dance. It is
discussed further in the chapter 3.

Though dance is our inheritance from Judaism, and it is certain that, as a Jew, Jesus danced, the persecutions of Christianity's early centuries worked to draw the early Christians away from these things. Concrete aspects of worship, which were shared with Judaism, such as dance, were "spiritualized" by some of the early leaders of the Church to draw a distinction between them and the Jews. In the second and third centuries, when persecutions were directed alternately at Christians and Jews, the Christians desired to differentiate themselves from the Jews, so they would not share in those persecutions that were aimed at their Jewish brothers and sisters!

Worship spaces

The first Christian worship spaces were private homes. In times and places where Christianity was prohibited, believers met secretly and had too little space for much more than speaking or singing. It was impractical to dance in such a worship space.

When Christians did not fear imminent danger in worshipping, they danced outdoors, and as space would permit, within their places of worship. But the persecutions of the early centuries took their toll on dance and, from a number of fronts, broke the chain of tradition from Judaism to Christianity in this aspect of worship.

Pagan influences

Another dancing spirituality is Paganism. Our inheritance from them is considerable and often deliberately overlooked. If you have ever danced around a May pole, decorated a pine tree in the winter (solstice), or colored eggs (a potent fertility symbol) at the Spring Equinox, you have participated in something which was once a Pagan ritual. Early Christianity borrowed heavily and shamelessly from Paganism, a religion based on respect for the earth.

Somewhere in the early centuries of Christianity, people of ANY religion other than Christianity were labelled "pagan," thus I use Pagan as a proper noun and pagan as an adjective. The word "pagan" later took on connotations of evil and through the centuries, became synonymous with Satan worship in some Christian circles. This is simply a misconception. Satan worship is Satan worship; it defines itself in opposition to Christianity, which means it cannot pre-date Christianity. Paganism is much older and does not consider Christianity in defining itself.

As people converted from Judaism, Paganism, and other religions, they brought their dances, which had significant spiritual meaning for them. People from many spiritual traditions wished to take the dances which had inspired them in their youth and find a way to make these dances part of their new spirituality as Christians. With some dance this was possible. Christianity has a long history of "baptizing" the stories, rituals, and celebrations from other traditions, by changing a few ideas and names, and using them to the enrichment of Christianity.

Baptism itself is an example of this! Symbolic washings were part of Judaism and many other religions. Our eucharist is rooted in the Jewish Passover, which Jesus was celebrating at his last supper. Many religions have flood stories and some are as old as the Hebrew story. The *Epic of Gilgamesh* was written around 1750 BCE, at the time of the Jewish patriarchs. So obviously Christians were not shy about borrowing rituals or stories!

Simple dances were reinterpreted to carry Christian themes. Others, however, such as the fertility rites of Beltane, could never become appropriate expressions of Christian spirituality. The tricky part was deciding which could be used and which could not. This generated a great deal of tension in those early years and continues to do so today!

Christian leaders had much on their minds, trying to strengthen the voice of this young religion, develop its creeds and doctrines, while discerning and eliminating unacceptable practices. Unfortunately leaders often found it easier to prohibit certain practices, such as dance, altogether, rather than trying to sort the worthy from the unworthy additions, as physical expressions of Christian piety took hold among the laity.

Clericalism

In its earliest days Christianity was led primarily by common people (Paul being a notable exception). Jesus had gone out of his way to recruit disciples who were thought to be some of the least powerful or worthy members of his society. Most were uneducated and extremely unlikely spiritual leaders. He did not recruit leaders for the Chrisitian movement from those who were already trained in Jewish tradition and law, such as the Pharisees or Saducees. Rather, he recruited smelly, illiterate fishermen. Many of his followers were women. Almost without exception, these were people who did not hold power in the eyes of their contemporaries. These were people who had the ability to love and trust their God as children trust their parents.

These were people who did not set out immediately to develop a systematic theology or reproduce the many laws of Judaism in their newfound relationship with God. Jesus found some of the most exuberant, excitable people he could--people who said and did things impulsively and spoke out of turn (just think of Simon Peter!). These were people who laughed and danced and told others about God's love in the simplest terms they could find. That was what Jesus chose. (Luke 18:17 Truly I tell you, whoever does not receive the kingdom of God as a little child will never enter it). He sought out people with intense, child-like faith who would die for what they believed, because in the coming years, many would. But that would all change with Constantine.

In the years between Jesus' crucifixion and Constantine's ascent to power, the Christian movement had grown in a way which frightened many political leaders, making it a target for varying degrees of official persecution. Out of the blood of its martyrs grew a Christian Church full of faith, determination, and passion. It was led by women and men who preached Jesus' message of God's love and gave themselves completely to God's will. Though some hierarchy had formed, it was greatly overshadowed in political power and influence by the emperors of Rome, rulers who worshiped the gods of Rome.

Then, in the early fourth century, the leadership of the Roman Empire was shaken up. Constantine was the son of Constantius. His rival, Maxentius, was the son of Diocletian's colleague, Maximian, who had usurped power in Italy and North Africa. It is important to note that Diocletian was one of the nastiest persecutors of Christianity. The showdown between the armies of these two men came to a place called the Mulvian Bridge, across the Tiber River. In this place a miracle occurred for the young Christian Church.

Constantine made a decision which would change the course of history. He decided to trust the God of the Christians and had the Chi-Rho painted on his soldiers' shields. Constantine won this decisive battle. It didn't take long for him to consolidate power and become sole ruler of the empire. Though he accepted the pagan title, "Pontifex Maximus," and the coinage still contained the Sun God, Constantine gave Christianity full legal equality with other religions, including the cult of Rome, and restored all properties confiscated in the persecutions under Diocletian. The year was 313 of the Common Era. A new day dawned for Christianity, as its power became forever entwined with secular power. This is the turning point, where Christianity went from a humble, struggling, movement, full of people ready to die for their convictions, to a powerful state religion, full of people seeking a variety of ends, not all of them consistent with the Gospel of Jesus, the Messiah.

One result of this development should have been a lovely, spacious place for dance, as grand worship spaces were eventually built with tax money. But this would not be the case. The new power given to the clergy caused a chasm to develop between them and the common worshippers.

Symbolically, this can be seen in the way in which the worship leaders' seating, together with the altar, was moved from the center of the congregation to a distant area at the front of the worship space, which was usually elevated. The gap between clergy and worshippers widened further as the mass continued in Latin, though it was increasingly NOT the language of common people. Dancing was discouraged. It was far too empowering to worshippers. It linked them directly to the divine without the intermediary role of the clergy. Doug Adams writes:

> The Catholic Hierarchy knew all too well the power of literal group dance. The Catholic objection to popular participation in dance reveals a political dimension of dancing. The superior position which clergy in the Catholic Church maintained over their laity had required that dancing together be suppressed as too equalizing and revolutionary. (Adams, p. 35)

Christian worship suffered losses in the laity's participation, as dance, congregational singing, and even the taking of wine during eucharist were taken away. For the laity, worship would become more of a spectator sport than an exercise of the whole person--but not forever. The proponents of dance would never give up. In each generation, people would challenge what the Church was becoming. Dance was far too powerful to be locked out forever.

Dances of the People

Throughout the next centuries and into the Middle Ages, common dances and other creative expressions of individual faith were discouraged by a largely elitist clergy. The gap between the upper and lower classes widened and the life of the peasants, to borrow a phrase from Hobbes, became "nasty brutish, and short."

The Church in Europe was central to social as well as religious life. People had a love-hate relationship with the Church structure, on one hand looking to it in an almost superstitious way for passage into a better afterlife, and on the other hand, resenting the clergy, who owned land and had a much easier life than the peasants. Often there were abuses and priests were unfit for a variety of reasons (not receiving proper education, buying or inheriting the role of priest, with no sense of divine calling, etc.), deepening the resentment of the commoners.

At a time when it was necessary for church councils to explicitly prohibit beer drinking and commercial trade within the churchyard, it is not difficult to imagine that all physical expressions (which may have included hand gestures and public urination) toward the church were not reverent or worshipful. Thus, bans on dancing are not surprising. It was easier for ecclesial authorities to simply ban all dancing than to differentiate between appropriate/worshipful and inappropriate dance.

Still, there were dances which would not be stifled by anyone's proclamation. Dance speaks when words fail and when grief or joy cannot be contained. Dance has power. When people are faced with God, whether in the form of beauty and miracle, or death and pain, they create song, art, and dance. Dance has been highly regarded throughout nearly all ages and cultures for its power to heal, whether that be in literal terms or only in spirit.

One dance, born in pain, which could not be suppressed by the Church, was the "Danse des Mortes" or "Danse Macabre." This "dance of death" symbolized death in the form of the plagues which swept through Europe, touching the lives of all. From the twelfth through the sixteenth centuries this was the most widely known religious dance in that part of the globe. It was especially popular from 1347-1373 when the Black Death, a combination of bubonic and pneumonic plagues, ravaged Europe. People yearned to seize this evil thing which took their mothers, their brothers, their friends, and drive it off so it could kill no more. Evil was personified by a single dancer as "the devil" and a dance was created, where the source of the evil and disease was symbolically caught and exorcised. It was danced in Italy, Spain, France, Germany, England, and Switzerland. It is evidenced in numerous wall paintings and much literature. It was often performed in churchyards.

Another dance, which is widely remembered, is the Mozarabe. This seventh century dance involved "a wooden arc of the Testament carried through the cathedral in procession, accompanied by choir-boys and priests. They were preceded by eight boys dancing and singing and dressed as angels with garlands of flowers in their hair." (Daniels pp. 22-23)

After many centuries of performance, it was forbidden in 1439 by Don Jayme de Palafox, the Archbishop of Seville. The dance was such a beloved part of the people's worship that the people of Seville collected money and sent the young dancers to Rome to dance the Mazarabe before Pope Eugenius IV. The pope responded, "I see nothing in this children's dance which is offensive to God. Let them continue before the high altar." (Daniels p. 23)

Church Fathers

As with many aspects of Christian theology and worship, dance has been reviled by some and embraced by others. While some Christian leaders thought dance to be at best unnecessary and at worst, destructive, other great men of influence within the Church have loved and promoted dance as a form of worship, defending it from many false perceptions. In the second century, Lucian of Samosata called dance "an act good for the soul, the interpretation of what is hidden in the soul." (Gagne p. 39)

In a late fourth century sermon on the text of Luke 7:32, Ambrose, the Bishop of Milan, gives this eloquent defense of dance:

> . . . the dance should be conducted as did David when he danced before the ark of the Lord, for everything is right which springs from the fear of God. Let us not be ashamed of a show of reverence which will enrich the cult and deepen the adoration of Christ. For this reason the dance must in no wise be regarded as a mark of reverence for vanity and luxury, but as something which uplifts every living body instead of allowing the limbs to rest motionless upon the ground or the slow feet to become numb . . . This dance is an ally of faith and an honoring of grace. The Lord bids us dance . . . . " (Daniels p. 18-19)

There are numerous references to dance as a beneficial and welcome part of liturgy in the early Church. Its proponents include Gregory of Nazianzus, Bishop of

Constantinople (circa 329-389); Gregory of Nyssa (335-394), who wrote of Jesus as the "Great Choreographer." Basil the Great (344-407), Bishop of Caesarea, wrote, "we remember those now, who together with the angels, dance the dance of the angels around God, just as in flesh they performed a spiritual dance of life . . . ." Jerome (340-407) saw dance as an expression of holy joy and the anticipation of heaven. Ambrose (397-440), requested that "persons about to be baptized approach the font dancing." Hippolytus and Clement are also among the Church Fathers who favored dance. These influential leaders judged dance according to its place in Scripture, tradition, and the hearts of the people. They encouraged sacred dance as an acceptable, even necessary, form of worship and praise.

Some of the later history is listed in the chart to follow. It is interesting to note that in the history of prohibitions against dance, we are given many glimpses of what types of dances were done and how pervasive dance seemed to be at many points in the Church's history.

A Brief History of Dance in Christian Worship

I have found it most helpful when explaining Christianity's ambivalent approach to dance throughout history, to show a timeline with two categories: one showing Christianity's use of dance and the other showing its prohibitions of the same. With the exception of the first couple entries on each side, this list is condensed from a larger list of events in the chapter entitled "Chronology of Liturgical Dance (300-1800) and the Events which Shaped attitudes about Liturgical Dance" in the book, *Introducing Dance in Christian Worship* by Ronald Gagne, Thomas Kane, and Robert VerEecke.

FAVOR DANCE

1st Century: dance is incorporated into Christian worship from Jewish worship. Dance, in the Talmud, is described as one of the principle functions of the angels

120 Acts of John describes dancing at the Last Supper.

150 Justin Martyr writes in support of dance

OPPOSE DANCE

1st-4th Centuries persecutions lead Christians to "spiritualize" Jewish traditions such as dancing. The lack of space, when meeting secretly in believers' homes, also makes dance very difficult

306-337 Dance is discouraged during the reign of Constantine.

FAVOR DANCE	OPPOSE DANCE
2nd Century: Lucian of Samosata describes dance as "an act good for the soul" and Clement of Alexandria writes of holy choral dances	367 Epiphanius, Bishop of Salamis, writes that dance involving both men and women is bound to lead to promiscuity
215 Hippolitus of Rome uses the image of dance to describe Christ's actions in his Easter hymn of praise	345-407 John Crysostom writes that it is unseemly that we should jump around like camels
264-339 Eusebius of Caesarea tells how Christians danced to praise God after the victory of Constantine	354-430 Augustine approves only of "spiritualized" dance. He uses it as a sermon illustration, but doesn't want people actually doing it
335-394 Gregory of Nyssa writes of Jesus as the Great Choreographer	470-542 Caesarius of Arles calls dance "sordid and disgraceful"
344-407 Basil the Great writes, "we remember those now, who together with the angels, dance the dance of the angels around God, just as in flesh they performed a spiritual dance of life . . .."	539 Council of Toledo forbids singing and dancing at the Festival of Fools
	743 Council of Lessinas forbids dancing of laymen and singing of nuns

FAVOR DANCE

340-420 Jerome saw dance as an expression of holy joy and the anticipation of heaven

397-440 Ambrose requested that persons about to be baptized approach the font dancing

827-844 Pope Gregory IV shows appreciation of dance by the inauguration of the Children's Festival

900 Theophylactus, the Patriarch of Constantinople, introduces dance in churches or before the altar on Christmas and Epiphany

1200 Chartres, France, a cathedral is constructed with a labyrinth in the floor, often used for dancing

OPPOSE DANCE

826 Council of Rome forbids women to sing or perform choir dances

900 Regino, Abbot of Prium, forbids dancing in churchyards and death watches

1170 Balsamon, Patriarch of Antioch, formulates proscriptions against dancing in churches of Constantinople, where they were performed on January 6, the Day of the Three Kings

1198 Bishop of Paris forbids the Festival of Fools in French churches

1206 Synod of Cahors threatens with excommunication any who dance inside or in front of churches

FAVOR DANCE

ca. 1250 William Durandus, Bishop of Mende, describes the "pilota" dance in his handbook on the mass

1248-1275 Eudes Rigaud, Archbishop of Rouen, records in his journal that in Villarceaux, cloistered nuns danced on the Feast of the Holy Innocents and priests danced on the Feast of Saint Nicholas

1264 Pope Urban IV creates Corpus Christi procession in which people are to participate with dances

1347-1373 Danse des Mortes popular as plague ravages Europe

1350 Sacred dances given on Maundy Thursday and Good Friday in a church in Florence, Italy

OPPOSE DANCE

1227 Council of Trier (Germany) forbids three-step and ring dances in churches and churchyards

1298 Council of Wurzburg (again Germany) threatens heavy punishment and describes dances at night watches and the saints' feasts as a grievous sin

1435 Council of Bale tries to prohibit ring dances and plays in churches and churchyards

1518 Council of Strasburg proscribes that music accompany dance in church on account of the dancing epidemic; but the Council specifically states that this prohibition does not apply to the common custom of the priest performing a sacral dance to special music at his first mass

FAVOR DANCE

1439 Pope Eugenius IV, in a Papal Bull, authorizes the "seises" (choir boy dances) for the Seville Cathedral

1436-1517 Cardinal Ximenes restored the Mozarabic Rite (performed in 678)

1453 the Dance of Death is performed in the Church of Ste. Jean in Besancon, France

1478 round dance is performed during Easter Mass in a church in Hildshem, Germany

1500 King of Portugal and his court dance the "Gloria" of the Mass on Christmas morning

1502-1534 Gil Vicente writes plays used in popular religious and courtly festivities, usually incorporating music and dance

OPPOSE DANCE

1547 Parliament of Paris prohibits the custom of music and dance at the first Mass of a new priest

1565 Synod of Compostella (Italy) forbids dances and plays during Mass, but the prohibition was soon withdrawn

1566-67 Council of Lyons excommunicates priests and laity who lead dances in the churches or cemeteries

1570 Council of Mechlin (Belgium) seeks to induce the civil authorities to prevent such dances as might seduce the congregation at Mass

1617 Archbishop of Cologne forbids dances in church by the bride and groom after the marriage ceremony and by the congregation at large

FAVOR DANCE

1555 Saint Teresa dances at Carmel

1582 In the book of rites of the Church of Ste. Marie Magdeleine, a dance called the "bergeratta" is described. It was performed in the churches of the diocese of Besacon, France

1609 A processional dance in celebration of the canonization of Ignatius of Loyola in Loreto, Italy

1610 "Ballet Ambulatoire" is performed to celebrate the canonization of Cardinal Charles Borromeo

1619 Jesuits organize a two day theatrical presentation for the reception of King Philip III of Spain and Portugal, including music and dance

OPPOSE DANCE

1665 Public festivities of music and dance in Portugal are controlled by law (a permit is necessary)

1667 Parliament of Paris forbids religious dances in general and particularly the public dances of Jan 1 and May 1, the torch dances of the first Sunday in Lent and those held around bonfires on the Vigil of St. John

1716 Bishop of Lisbon renews interdiction concerning plays and dances inside churches, although the Corpus Christi procession remains untouched

1753 The Bishop of Barcelona forbids the "eagle dance" in churches.

FAVOR DANCE

1634 A "moral ballet" is composed to commemorate the birthday of the Cardinal of Savoy

1682 Jesuit, Pere Menestrier of Paris publishes book on dancing in the Christian Church

OPPOSE DANCE

1777 A royal decree of Madrid seeks to prevent all dancing on holy days in churches or churchyards

1780 Spain: A royal decree states that no dances would be performed in churches of the realm

Grace Lutheran Church, Easter 2000. The three dancers visible are Adrianna Greising, Kyra Borchers, and Denise J. Miller. Photo by Deena Sherman

Chapter 3
Scripture

If you have considered dancing in Christian worship, you may have done a search, either by computer or simple concordance, to find the references to dance in Christian scripture. I will list them below. The first thought for many who do this is--as it was for me--why aren't there more?! If dance was part of Jewish and early Christian worship, why isn't it talked about more?

I puzzled over this, then I realized something. Scripture doesn't talk about the attire of the clergy. It doesn't outline early liturgies. It doesn't list popular songs early Christians sang. It doesn't note that as time progressed, the cross became a central symbol and held a prominent place in worship spaces. It doesn't often note making the sign of the cross on one's chest to remember one's baptism. You see where I'm going with this? Some things are so common that they are simply taken for granted. If you are describing a soccer game, you don't note that the goalies are dressed differently from the other players or that both feet must be on the ground on a throw in. Everybody knows that! If you said or wrote that in your commentary of a game, people would look at you funny!

First, let's look at those writings we inherited from our Jewish brothers and sisters, which we label the "Old Testament." They were originally written in Hebrew (the official language for writing and scholarship) and Aramaic (the everyday language Jesus spoke), except for cussing, which was done in other people's languages, so as not to sully their own. I love that and think of it every time I borrow words from my German or French ancestors when I'm frustrated.

Anyway, in Aramaic, the words for "dance" and "rejoice" are the same (Adams p. 16). For those people, rejoicing almost always involved dancing.

Here my children demonstrate how rejoicing often means spontaneously dancing. In this 1996 photo, the children react to the new hardwood floor which had just been installed to replace the one we lost in a major flood. Photo by Deena Sherman.

We see this particular word carry over into Christian scripture when in Matthew 5:11-12 we see the word "rejoice." Luke's parallel passage, chapter 6 verses 22-23, uses "leap for joy." That sounds like dancing to me! Luke simply makes it clearer for his non-Jewish audience that rejoicing means leaping about, or dancing, just in case some uptight Gentiles don't get that.

In Hebrew there are over 40 words for dancing, only one is specifically for secular dance; the remaining 39 are for sacred dance. From this we may readily conclude that dance was important, varied, and used for God.

The references to dance in the writings which became the Christian Bible sometimes do no more than reinforce the fact that dance was definitely a part of life for Israel and for early Christians. People, who rejoiced before God, danced. Here are all of the places the specific word "dance" is mentioned in scripture.

Judges 11:29-40 tells the unfortunate story of Jephthah's vow. His daughter is the first to come out to meet him after he wins a battle against the Ammonites. As one would expect, in her joy over her father's success, she is dancing. Sadly he has made a vow, which I cannot fathom, to kill the first person who comes out the doors of his house to greet him in exchange for God giving him victory! One would think it more prudent to offer something of oneself to God when making a vow, not the lives of loved ones!

Judges chapter 21 tells the almost comic story of the Benjaminites being saved from extinction by kidnapping brides from the women of Shiloh who come out to dance! This does little more than remind us that dance was a common part of life in that time.

In Exodus 15:19-21 Miriam (Aaron's sister) dances after the crossing of the Red (or actually Reed) Sea. Where there is rejoicing, there is dancing!

1 Samuel 18:6 tells of women coming out to sing and dance for joy when King David returned home from killing Goliath. Again, when there is rejoicing, there is dancing. Chapters 21 verse 12 and 29 verse 5 make reference to this, noting again that dancing accompanied the songs of David's deed.

In I Samuel 30:16 it is King David's enemies who are eating, drinking, and dancing to celebrate a raid of Ziklag. David kills most of them. This doesn't tell us much except that Israel wasn't the only people of that time who rejoiced over slaughtering their enemies and who danced when rejoicing.

2 Samuel 6:14-23 is one of the most commonly cited passages about God approving of dance. Here King David dances for joy as the Ark of God is brought into Jerusalem. This passage may be particularly satisfying for dancers who encounter criticism of dance in worship, since the person who is David's most vocal detractor, is punished by God! Michal, Saul's daughter, calls David and his dance "vulgar" and "shameless." She is struck barren.

The Book of Psalms notes dance in Psalm 30 ("You have turned my mourning into dancing"), 149, and 150. Both 149 and 150 specifically speak of dance as a worthy way in which to show praise for God. "Let Israel be glad in its Maker; let the children of Zion rejoice in their King. Let them praise his name with dancing . . . " (149:2-3) and "Praise him with trumpet sound; praise him with lute and harp! Praise him with tambourine and dance; praise him with strings and pipe!" (150:3-4)

Ecclesiastes chapter 3 is familiar to most. "For everything there is a season, and a time for every purpose under heaven." (3:1 KJV) Verse 4 affirms that there is "A time to weep, and a time to laugh; a time to mourn, and a time to dance."

Lamentations 5:15 "The joy of our hearts has ceased; our dancing has been turned to mourning."

Moving on to the gospel accounts, Matthew 11:17 (mirrored in Luke 7:32) isn't very helpful for our purposes. Jesus criticizes his audience, likening them to children who call to one another, "We played the flute for you, and you did not dance . . . " It does, however, serve to reinforce once again, the pervasiveness of dance in Jesus' world.

Matthew 14 tells of the dance of Heriodias' daughter, which won her the head of John the Baptist. This is obviously NOT *sacred* dance.

Luke 15:25 notes the dancing which accompanied the music for the party when the prodigal son returned home. Rejoicing=dancing.

If we look to other ancient writings, we find much more detail about dance. In the mid-second to third centuries C.E., Justin Martyr and Hippolytus speak of dance, as does Eusebius, a prominent early church historian. But one of the most fascinating pieces of writing about dance in the early church is found in the Acts of John (120 C.E.), an apocryphal Gnostic writing. It is quoted in the Catholic Dictionary as being known to Augustine and describes dancing at the Last Supper. The disciples gather around Jesus and perform a circle dance, with Jesus speaking the words, "whoso danceth not, knoweth not the way of life. Now answer thou to my dancing. Behold thyself in my who speak, and seeing what I do, keep silence about my mysteries." (Sorrell p. 20-21, Daniels p.

14) There is far more to our Christian heritage than what we find bound between Genesis and Revelation. While many apocryphal writings have shortcomings, which show us why they were not judged worthy of the canon, they can still give us intriguing glimpses into our past.

Dancing at Faith Lutheran Church in Brookfield, Il 1995
Photo by Rev. Eric Deffenbaugh

But to apprehend
The point of intersection of the timeless
With time, is an occupation for the saint--
No occupation either, but something given
And taken, in a lifetime's death in love,
Ardour and selflessness and self-surrender.
For most of us, there is only the unattended
Moment, the moment in and out of time,
The distraction fit, lost in a shaft of sunlight,
The wild thyme unseen, or the winter lightening
Or the waterfall, or music heard so deeply
That it is not heard at all, but you are the music
While the music lasts. These are only hints and guesses,
Hints followed by guesses; and the rest
Is prayer, observance, discipline, thought and action.
The hint half guessed, the gift half understood, is
Incarnation.
Here the impossible union
Of spheres of existence is actual,
Here the past and future
Are conquered, and reconciled . . . .

--T.S. Eliot
Four Quartets

Chapter 4
Embodiment

Dancing at Faith Lutheran Church in Brookfield, IL 1995
Photo by Rev. Eric Deffenbaugh

Since Christianity's founding, it has been ambivalent about the issue of embodiment. Bodies scare us. They're high-maintenance, demanding, smelly, imperfect parts of our humanity. The idea that God chose to inhabit one of these, through Jesus, is no less than scandalous! The exact nature of God's embodiment in the person of Jesus fueled many a debate, schism, and convened many an official Council in the early centuries of Christianity's development. The tension between human embodiment and holy transcendence is an ongoing dilemma for Christians, who strive to understand their God, themselves, and their mission.

The culture which cradled infant Christianity was decidedly dualistic. In this world everything is divided into neat categories of light and darkness, good and bad, body and spirit, male and female. This is derived from parts of Plato's thinking. Unfortunately, Paul, Augustine, and other early Christian leaders found this worldview quite attractive and tried to impose it upon Christianity. St. Augustine believed that Platonism was a "preliminary and necessary step in the acceptance of Christianity." (Reese p. 443)

In this dualistic thinking, the rational is good, the physical is evil. Men are, of course, rational, while women who live in the physical realm of childbearing, are obviously evil, or at best, vessels for tempting men away from rational, intellectual, godly pursuits. Women were of the flesh, men of the spirit. (See James Nelson's book, *Embodiment*)

This tendency to "spiritualize" aspects of worship and set up this body-versus-soul dichotomy has been the single greatest obstacle to dance. It has also been a destructive force within Christianity in general, keeping us from more holistic view of worship and our relationship with God. There has been a long and unfortunate confusion in Christianity between the blessings of using our senses to worship as whole person and the idea of our senses drawing us away from God toward lewd behavior. One does not automatically lead to the other.

In fear, we risk throwing out the baby with the bathwater, so to speak. In trying to make the Church righteous enough for God's presence, we can be tempted to chop away parts of our humanity. We hear this suggested in Matthew 5:27-30 and wonder exactly how to respond:

" . . . But I say to you that everyone who looks at a woman with lust has already committed adultery with her in his heart. If your right eye causes you to sin, tear it out and throw it away; it is better for you to lose one of your members than for your whole body to be thrown into hell . . . . "

Notice this passage asks people to take personal responsibility for their feelings of lust. It does not say to harm the person or thing which is perceived to cause that person to lust! Perhaps if we, as Christians, took this passage more literally—the personal responsibility part, not the eye plucking—we would take the opportunity to examine ourselves more critically and grow in faith rather than plucking out the people or worship forms we fear will provoke us to unclean thinking. But it's so much easier to prohibit anything and everything which runs the slightest risk of offense, rather than taking personal responsibility for our lusts or thoughts. It is easier to put things into neat little boxes and throw some away than to examine ourselves in any deep and meaningful way. The price of the neat little boxes is that there is no room for exceptions to the rules and certainly no room for the idea of paradox.

Unfortunately for those who wished to move from the predominant thinking of their culture into the thinking of the newborn Christian movement, the paradox of a God who is incarnated as a man, who is spirit and flesh in One Being is essential to understanding who Jesus is! Incorporating that into the worldview of the predominant culture would take nearly a miracle. It would take extreme intellectual gymnastics to embrace this new understanding of God, but the great thinkers of the Church's early centuries embraced the challenge. In a simpler time, with no mass media to distract them, they diligently set to the task of debating, postulating, further debating, and eventually formulating Christian theology--then debating it some more.

As early Christian leaders and thinkers tried to wrap their minds around this idea of God's embodiment, there were clearly some false starts. One of these was the idea that Jesus only appeared to be human but never really was. This idea would become the heresy of Docetism. It's easy to see why this idea was attractive. It would seem beneath God to take on actual human flesh! Think about it. We don't really want to think about Jesus sweating, belching, having bad breath, being completely human as we are! It's easier to think of the incarnation as God on holiday, slumming with the mortals for a little while. He looked like a Jewish carpenter by day, but underneath, there was really always a big G on his chest. The angels probably came to wash his feet and comb his hair in the evenings to make him look like the famous Warner Sallman "Head of Christ" painting.

I believe Christianity still has a great number of closet Docetists. I can tell by the pictures of a Swedish-looking Jesus with the celestial halo hovering over neatly combed light brown hair and big blue eyes. His skin is milky white. We can say Jesus was truly man all we like, but often our art does not reflect this.

Erring to the opposite extreme were the Arians. This is a tricky word. Spelled with a Y (Aryan), it was the name of the "race" of people in the theories of Adolf Hitler. This word has nothing to do with that. These were simply people who followed a presbyter from Baucalis, near Alexandria (in Egypt), named Arius. Around 318 C.E. Arius began teaching that Jesus was created out of nonexistence, as humans are. He did not exist from the beginning with God. Jesus could be completely human because he was not fully divine.

Again, you can see how this is attractive. It saves us from blurring the lines between divine and human and gets around the paradox of God choosing to be fully human in the person of Jesus of Nazareth. Christology (coming to an understanding of who Jesus is) is a tough undertaking, but absolutely essential.

Sacred dance, bringing the physical into worship, can be difficult for Christians to embrace for some of the same reasons that Christology prompted so much debate in the early church: we like easy answers and we like our humanity and divinity separate. There is something very fundamentally frightening about the idea of God choosing to become fully human, with all that entails. There is also something frightening about using our bodies in the act of worshipping. It's hard enough to hold onto the idea of a God of paradox! To ask us to do that, plus ask us to decide--case by case, day by day-- what things bring us closer to this God or pull us away from him, is brutally difficult! It puts a number of burdens and responsibilities on the Christian.

Thus, the appeal of dualistic thinking is easy to understand. It takes a world full of messy situations, relationships, and aspects of being human and divides it all into good and bad, spirit and body, yes and no. It takes truths, half-truths, and choices where "right" is not always apparent, and reduces it to neat little boxes where everything is clear. It takes away all that nasty hard work! No longer must we trouble ourselves to struggle with blacks and whites which are sometimes really grey. We become the Pharisees who would prohibit Jesus from healing on the Sabbath because it breaks "God's law."

Separating the spiritual "mandate" from the physical, concrete results of a decision can not only cause us to lose opportunities to reflect God's grace, but can also blind us to the potential for damage. Separating the Spirit of the law from the letter of the law can turn good intentions in to evil actions. What begins with a commitment to fighting for what we believe is right, if taken to an extreme, can become the very incarnation of evil! The most glaring example I can think of is when I hear of people on the radical fringe of the pro-life movement, who kill doctors to achieve their goal of "saving children!"

Another example from history comes from the fourth crusade. In 1212 several thousand children set out for Palestine. They had great faith that they did this for God. They were shipwrecked and died or were sold into slavery, all for the glory and political ambitions of the Church. Such stories of good intentions gone wrong are not easy to think about. They grey areas of life are not a comfortable place, so many people simply choose not to believe they exist. There are a lot of days I wish I could do that too! But, as we all know, those who do not learn from the errors of history are doomed to repeat them or be victimized by them!

Why, you may ask, do I examine these heresies and pieces of history in talking about sacred dance? Because the types of thinking which led to these, still exists in parts of the Christian family. We seldom take time to debate the exact nature of the trinity these days, but our beliefs about these things have a real impact upon the judgements we make about how we act and how we worship, including whether to include dance.

While many other religions view dance as a sacred act and very much worthy of God's presence, even essential in God's praise, Christians are often squeamish. We are fine with the concrete elements of bread and wine becoming body and blood. We feel the tangible water of baptism and understand its transcendent power, yet when we see dance, too often we see only flesh, only our humanity, not the spark of divinity which God offers us as we become vessels in a creative gift in the dance!

Remember the man from Wisconsin I mentioned in chapter 1 who was afraid to look at the dance which I had done to accompany the L.S.T.C. Choir? While I was disappointed at the time that this person was not able to receive a blessing from that dance, I had to respect the fact that this man was absolutely honest and had made the choice which he felt was right for him--not to look. It was too frightening for him and he acted accordingly. To this day I treasure that image he painted of the breeze blowing by him--like God's Spirit. A woman near him, however, raved about how much the dance added to the choir concert. The man had done the right thing. He let this woman, and others in that place, be blessed by the offering of dance. He did not ask that it be stopped. He did not complain that it was done, he simply admitted that he wasn't ready to see it. I am forever grateful to those with such an attitude!

Too many times I have heard the argument that dance is inappropriate because it does not show proper respect for God. If we worshipped a God who sat on a throne somewhere out of our reach, waiting to smell our burnt offerings in tribute to him, I might agree. But we worship a God who chose to take human form in the person of Jesus of Nazareth. He chose to eat and sleep, work and get splinters from the wood of his trade. He felt anger, sadness, and joy, and he sometimes danced, as Jewish men do, in celebration.

Where do we get the idea that God only wants us to sit still, be quiet and contemplate his glory? Who told us we could not express our joy or sorrow with words and movement? We may think we get this from pieces of scripture, taken out of context. "Be still and know that I am God (Psalm 46:10)" jumps first into my mind. Does this apply to dance? Look at the rest of the passage. Are we talking about dance here? No, we're talking about war. For any passage we might point to, if we look at it in context, it is not specifically prohibiting dance. There are no scripture passages which explicitly prohibit dance in worship. Keep in mind the one person who openly prohibits worshipful dance in scripture (see 2 Samuel 6:14-23) is punished by God with barrenness!

Here is a little more food for thought regarding scripture. In Matthew 19:13 we read: "Let the little children come to me and do not stop them; for it is to such as these that the kingdom of heaven belongs." Maybe this is just my experience, but the little children I know, when they are happy, make loud joyful noises, dance impulsively, and laugh loudly. They are certainly capable of containing themselves, but I still catch them dancing innocently and spontaneously.

Back to the reasons why we may have the impression that dance does not belong in worship. Maybe we get this idea from the clergy. Of course, it would depend on which clergy you ask. Many priests, pastors, and lay leaders love and support dance in worship. Some priests feel dance is not only acceptable, but even necessary. Father Lucien Deiss writes:

For too long a time we have prayed, "Let us praise the Lord with dancing" (Psalm 150), and we have not danced. For too long a time we have sung, "Let us make music with timbrel and harp" (Psalm 149), but what have we really done? We have removed all timbrels and harps from our churches, and retained only those which make no music whatsoever! Thus, at least, we have not run the risk of waking the people who sleep. (Diess, p. 8)

Others, from the early days of the Church onward, have feared dance. In the late fourth century we hear Basil of Caesarea and John Crysostom, Bishop of Constantinople, condemning dance for reasons of provoking lust in the onlookers. Christians are cautioned against dances at weddings and feasts, calling women who participate in them "harlots." Chrysostom writes, "Where there is dancing, there is the devil. It was not for this that God gave us feet, but that we might walk orderly . . . " (Davies p. 20).

Another of the early Church leaders, Epiphanius (315-403), Bishop of Salamis on Cypris, writes that dance involving both men and women is bound to lead to promiscuity (Ibid.)

Today I hear some leaders echo these prohibitions, saying dance is inappropriate, secular, not scriptural (in spite of Scripture), or not part of our tradition (in spite of the history). A music director in Sandusky, Ohio once stated, jokingly, as we shared our frustration about people's ideas of tradition, "Didn't you know? Tradition is what ever I can personally remember!" This is unfortunately the way many worshippers see it. They do not want the traditions of the early Church, they want the traditions of the early twentieth century.

Leaders sometimes voice the fear that dance threatens order and piety. I wonder whether they are really saying that it threatens their authority and control over others (see Doug Adams' words in chapter 2 about this)

They say they fear it causes people to feel lust. As I repeatedly state throughout this book, the dancer's clothing must always be appropriate. The focus must always stay on God and the moment of worship.

Assuming a dancer is clothed in such a way, which would not, in a focussed worshipper, take that focus away from that worship, I have a few more thoughts about the attitude that all dance is inappropriate because it causes unclean thoughts. First, if unclean thoughts are that close to the surface, there are other issues, which should be addressed by the person who is offended. If one cannot enjoy the beauty of the human form (well covered), praising God, then what other things might that person be missing out on in God's creation due to this fear of being tempted away from God by things which intend the opposite? What personal weaknesses do they wish to blame on others? Once more, I refer them to Matthew 5:27-30 and the idea of personal responsibility. One might also read Matthew 7:3-5 about finding the speck in another's eye before taking the log from one's own eye.

Throughout Church history, we see two different styles of leadership within the Church. Some leaders serve out of a profound sense of calling. They live a life of **self-sacrificing love,** true to the nature of God himself. These are the church leaders who never lose their humility, who literally get their hands dirty. They are not afraid of hard work, whether that is physical, emotional, or intellectual. They are comfortable with their own authority as called and ordained ministers to God's people, thus they are not afraid of other people's opinions that might differ from their own. They are willing to explore how God works differently in other people's lives, finding ways of sharing the blessings that God brings to different people in different ways.

There is, however, another style of leadership. It is based in fear, sometimes leading to abuses of power. When those of this group feel their power is threatened, they grasp it more firmly, crushing all debate or dissent. It happens on the parish level; it happens in the larger Church. This has played out over and over through the centuries. I look at the history of burning--or at least excommunicating--scientists, mystics, reformers, and prophets. Copernicus, Galileo, Martin Luther, John Hus, Joan of Arc . . . . the list of my personal heroes is long and each was harassed or killed by the Church of my heritage!

We can look at the inquisitions, the crusades, the support of slavery, or any number of dark times in the Church. Or we can simply consider the recent scandals in the Church of priests and leader molesting children, and the lengths to which the Church leadership went to protect the perpetrators instead of the children. I have personally seen the damage this has done in people's lives and stood aghast at this evil personified by those perpetrators and their protectors. This may be the ultimate abuse of authority and the ultimate misunderstanding of one's role as God's representative on earth

Understand I do not stand outside and throw stones at the stained glass windows. I scream in frustration from within this institution that I want to cheer on as it reflects the God who was incarnate in Jesus the Christ, who embodied self-sacrificing love!

But in the culture of fear and hunger for power which is sometimes exhibited, it would seem that church leaders forget their place as servants and vessels. In Matthew 20 Jesus tells his disciples "You know that the rulers of the Gentiles lord it over them, and their great ones are tyrants over them. It will not be so among you; but whoever wishes to be great among you must be your servant . . . " (Mat. 20:25-26)

Those of us who are trained in theology and worship are to be vehicles for God to bring blessings to his people. The calling is not to preserve one's own job security or ensure one's own power! Church leaders do not own or control the sacraments or the worship people offer to their God, they facilitate these things.

At most Lutheran congregations (ELCA), it is announced before the sacrament that all who believe Christ is present in this gift are welcome to come and receive it. It is not for us, as flawed humans, to decide who is worthy or unworthy to receive it! We simply offer it and let God bless his people. It is the same with baptism; it should be the same with dance. The Holy Scripture calls us to dance. The Holy Spirit calls us to dance. No representative of Christ's Church should stand between God and his people as he bestows his blessing. It is simply not our place.

Christianity began with God taking on our dirty, fragile, human flesh. Christian worship began celebrating that event with dances and songs in a community of people who were willing to give up their lives to witness to the truth of God coming into flesh. Jesus' message was of an accessible, enfleshed God who taught with his own incarnation and self-sacrificing love. This was a laughing, dancing God who literally got dirt in his sandals to stoop down and reach to the poor and unloved. Somehow we have perverted the lessons of this God into wars, crusades, political ambitions. We have become, in so many times and places, NOT the body of Christ, but something which scarcely resembles our loving, dancing God. Writing prohibitions against forms of worship, such as sacred dance, should not even make it onto our agenda as we begin to examine our stewardship of God's Church!

Chapter 5
Getting Started

Lecturing at a Lutheran youth event in Norwalk, Ohio, 1994.
Photo by Daniel W. Borchers

As the person who wishes to introduce dance to your congregation, you have some work ahead of you. I pray that this book will help you in completing it. First, you must meet with the pastor to discuss why it is important and how dance should be presented in the local parish/congregation. You should explain why you feel led to begin this dance ministry. You should explain what experience you have with dance and what style of dancing you wish to lead. You will want to assure your pastor that movements will be appropriate, not suggestive. You should discuss what the dancers would wear. There will be no risqué costuming. Everything should be modest and in line with the style of the worship itself. It is important to meet with the pastor and other worship leaders Whenever dance is planned within a worship service, to be sure it fits well into the worship experience as a whole.

It may be helpful, when dancing is newly begun in a parish, to put into writing a mission statement (an example is noted later in this chapter) and a statement about how dance will function in worship.

It should include:

1. how often dance will occur
2. in what parts of worship it might be used (as a processional, with a psalm, as part of the message, etc.)
3. a description of leadership roles, such as who does choreography, who schedules rehearsals, who oversees auditions--if that is a prerequisite--and who makes decisions about age, experience, readiness, etc.
4. what information and educational opportunities will be provided for the worshippers prior to the dance
5. how the dancers will work with the music leaders

If including liturgical dance in your worship must pass a council vote, it will be very helpful to be able to show them paperwork such as this, so they know you have considered carefully all that this entails. Also include your mission statement when you prepare your paperwork for the church council. Be sure that when council, or any other decision making body discusses dance, a dance leader is present to answer questions and concerns.

It is vital to meet with one or more members of the music staff, as live music is the preferred way to accompany the dance. It is, of course, possible to use prerecorded music if the staff does not have the time or inclination to accompany dance. It is important however, no matter what music is used, to work at obtaining the support and blessing of the music staff.

If dance will be a regular part of worship, with live music, you must contact the musicians and set a regular time during music practices for dancers to attend. When dancers are not accustomed to live music or musicians are not accustomed to dance, it can be difficult to adjust to working together. When dancers and musicians begin working together, a metronome is indispensable. Use a metronome to set a tempo during the practice of all pieces of music which will incorporate dance.

When liturgical dance is presented to a congregation for the first time, it is important to inform the congregation of the long history of dance in Christian worship (see chapter 2) prior to the day when dance becomes a part of *their* worship. Communication is always an important aspect of beginning new things for most congregations. A presentation to adult bible study groups and an article in the congregation's newsletter are essential. If it is possible to focus an entire adult study group on this topic for a period of time, this will be even more helpful. The greater the volume of exposure and information, the better the chances of dance being integrated smoothly and bringing the greatest possible blessings to the worshipping community.

Whether you are bringing dance to a congregation for the first time or you have been doing it for years, there are some steps you must take when you prepare to offer a dance.

First you pray. That sounds simple. That sounds pious. That sounds like something you may think I feel obliged to say. That's not why I say it. I'm saying it because I've done it both ways and one doesn't work. I've learned from many years of experience that it is vital to spend time in prayer in order to dance effectively in worship. If I'm dancing with others, I must pray for them as well as for the congregation, the dance, and myself. It makes all the difference.

Then you get the music for the first dance you will offer. If you are working with a musician or group, ask someone to tape the music practice. Then you live with the music. You play it while you're doing dishes and ironing shirts. You get to know it completely. If you find that the tempo is not workable, you need to contact the musician and set a time to meet. You need to listen to the music being played and arrive at a tempo which will work for your dance. As noted above, a metronome is essential in this, as the musician can then simply write a little number in the corner of the page of music and know, without question, how the piece is to be played. Without this, the nervousness of the dancing day can translate into a lot of tension about the speed to which you had agreed. I tend to speed things up when I'm nervous. A few times a musician has shown me the marking on his or her page that we made when we rehearsed and I was surprised that I had wanted that pace. But I had and I later understood why, when I saw the dance on videotape and knew that if it had gone faster, it would not have looked right.

Next, check out the space you will be using. Spend time in it, pace it off, pray in it. Understand its limits and its opportunities. This can be difficult when you are dancing at an unfamiliar church and do not know when the space is available. If the site is near your home, it is well worth the phone call (to make an appointment) and extra trip to that place to spend time prior to the day of the first practice.

Meet with your dancers if you will be dancing with a larger group. Understand their skills. Understand why they dance. Talk about the dance you will be working on together. Encourage them to also pray for one another, for you, and for the people who will receive the dance. If possible, meet with them in the space where you will be dancing so that when the time for choreography comes, they may offer ideas.

Now comes the choreography. Different dancers do this in different ways. The method that usually works best for me is to work first in the space alone, then take the parts I had worked out in that space back home. I do not worry about having the whole thing finished. Then I meet with the dancers in the space, teach them what I had prepared so far and ask for input. They are usually proud to be able to do that, but do not want the burden of choreographing the whole dance. Your experience may be different.

Plan enough practice times to prepare a dance which does not look sloppy or hesitant. Dancers need to feel prepared and confident. Be sure you rehearse the full dance with the musician or musicians adequately also. Be clear about the signal used between the lead dancer and the lead musician to begin the music. If it is a hymn, be sure you are clear with the musician(s) how many verses are to be played! These things may seem obvious, but I mention them because, in working with many musicians over the years, I've encountered a problem with each of these issues at least once! The first time I danced with a group at my most recent home congregation, the organist and I had not set a signal. I had worked with the musicians at my previous church home for many years and did not even think to mention "my signal" to the new organist. My dancers were not even lined up when she began playing the hymn to which we would dance! One was still in the ladies room and came running toward the sanctuary as we began the dance! It was not one of my prouder moments!

On the day of the dance there should be an informative announcement in the worship bulletin, which tells about liturgical dance in general, plus a description of the particular dance they will see. Congregants are usually surprised and pleased to learn about the history of dance in worship. Most people are thrilled to add dance to regular Sunday worship as well as special occasions, when they realize they are conserving a part of worship, which has blessed Christians for many centuries.

When introducing dance to a congregation in which most of the members have not yet seen dance in worship, it is important to start with choreography which is simple and dignified, so the worshippers do not feel overwhelmed. The purpose of dance is to express the faith of the community as a whole. This cannot be done if the community cannot relate to the dance. See chapters 7 and 8 for suggestions. Elaborate fine art dance productions can come, but the introduction of dance should be simple, fitting gracefully into the existing worship service.

To make liturgical dance a regular part of worship in your congregation, you will need at least one committed person, with some dance background, who is willing to become a troupe leader. This person must invest time (the amount will depend upon the frequency of dance in worship) to work with your pastor and/or worship team and possibly other dancers, to prepare for dance to be integrated into the worship. This investment of time will include prayer, worship planning, choreography (created or found), and practice. If dance is to be successfully integrated into worship, the pastor must not only tolerate it, but actively, vocally, support it. The worship musician(s), if they are playing for the dance, should also support dance. Since this usually means making time for live rehearsals with dancers and providing practice tapes for the dancers to use (especially if the choreography will be original), it is very uncomfortable when musicians do not support liturgical dance. See the *Music* section in this chapter for information about specific time requirements. If there is ambivalence, consider alternatives to live music.

When a troupe leader is in place and the ordained and musical leadership of the congregation are prepared to support dance, dancers may be recruited. This can be done as part of a time and talent survey in the congregation or by simply including announcements about the formation of a liturgical dance group in the bulletin or church newsletter. The pastor often knows of members who study dance and can give suggestions for personal contacts. Having this new means of utilizing the gifts of worshippers will often bring members who are gifted in dance or have a strong appreciation for the arts, and have been only marginally active before, into a much greater involvement in their congregation.

When a group of dancers has come together, it is important to keep clear lines of communication between the leader, dancers, and parents. A schedule of practices and performances should be given to the member of the group as soon as possible. Depending on the frequency with which dance will be utilized in worship, this could be a monthly, quarterly, or annual schedule. The rules and expectations should be clearly stated. If dancers cannot participate in a performance when they miss a practice, this must be stated at the onset. It will be helpful to check with the pastor about general rules for building use (where food or drinks are allowed, where there is no running or horseplay, gum chewing, etc.). While these things may seem obvious, it is always better to state ALL expectations clearly to avoid misunderstandings later.

The group may wish to write a brief mission statement to make its goals clear. Such a statement might read:

The Rejoice Dancers of Grace Lutheran Church use their dance skills to:
- *bring glory to the name of God as revealed to us in Father, Son and Holy Spirit,*
- *bring blessings to the Grace congregation,*
- *and make God's name known to all who see us dance.*

It is helpful to name the group if it is to be referred to in bulletins and newsletters. This becomes absolutely imperative if there are to be multiple groups within the congregation. Rather that calling the groups "beginner," "intermediate," and "advanced," names such as "Hosanna" or "Rejoice" will help to avoid hurt feeling over not being in the most "advanced" group.

The group leader must assess the dancers' skills. When there is a great disparity in age and/or skill, it may be best to split the group into subgroups or form two distinct groups. If there are a large number of untrained volunteer dancers, the leader must decide how much dance training she is willing to provide. Will dance lessons be part of the program? Will there be a fee for lessons or is this a gift of time and talent to the congregation?

If time constraints or other obstacles do not allow the group leader to offer dance training for these willing but inexperienced volunteers, there are a number of options. Dancers who have the interest and energy for liturgical dance but lack training should always be allowed to participate. To deny them this opportunity would be elitist and would not be true to the history or spirit of dance in Christian worship.

There are at least three alternatives for solving this problem. First, dances can be planned which do not require a great deal of training. Some are offered in this book. If the dancers are able to begin training at a local dance school, they can look forward to later moving into another dance group. The congregation may wish to consider offering scholarships to local dance schools if quality liturgical dance in their worship is an ongoing priority. A third option is allowing one of the more advanced dance students from the group of trained dancers, if such a person exists, to provide some instruction to the younger group. The church might also consider hiring a dance instructor to work with their dance troupes on a regular basis.

If there are a number of skilled dancers in the congregation, find out how they see dance fitting into worship. Briefly explain the history of dance in Christian worship. If their training is in styles which may not be appropriate for Christian worship, be sure they clearly understand the expectations surrounding dance in worship. The dancers must always be clearly focussed on dancing as a gift to God, not a performance for their own aggrandizement. Thrusting or gyrating hips are not acceptable. The most helpful dance training is in classical ballet or folk dance. If the most experienced dancers learn to effectively channel their talent into dance which benefits the worshipping community, they will become a valuable resource in planning choreography and possibly helping to train the younger dancers.

Since liturgical dance can be done in many ways by a range of groups, including variations in age and levels of training and experience, the following chapters will address the issues of working with different types of liturgical dance groups in a variety of worship settings.

Music

One will find a wide variety of musical styles within Christian worship. This might include anything from pipe organ to a country western or rock style band. As stated above, dancers need the cooperation of church musicians if liturgical dance is to be performed with live music, which is generally preferable. When the musicians practice, a tape can easily be made of the song which is to be used for the dance on portable recording equipment (a "boom box"). If the church uses a mixing board, and recordings can be made directly from that, it will vastly improve the sound quality of the practice tape.

It is important for the musicians and dancers to practice adequately together prior to a performance. As noted above, the musicians must take great care to recreate the same tempo that they used on the practice tape the dancers used (see passages about using a metronome). If the pace becomes significantly faster or slower, the results can range from frustrating to regrettable.

Plan at least **one hour** of time for choreography and another **hour** of practice time **for every minute** of non-repeating music being choreographed. When there are refrains, or if choreography repeats with each new verse, do not calculate choreography time for those parts of the music. Don't forget to allow the dancers time to warm up before practicing. See pages the end of this chapter for sample warm up exercises.

The specific pieces of music, which are chosen for dance, should be worshipful. This usually, but not always, excludes secular music.

Carefully look at the music you wish to use, if it is not from a source of church music, with your pastor. The music should never detract from the worship by radically changing the flow of the rest of the service and leaving the congregation to wonder why this odd element was inserted. While the music can be exuberant and interesting, it should never be irreverent. If there are lyrics, they should focus on our relationship with God and, if possible, reflect the theme of the day's worship.

For example: I have choreographed to the music, "People Get Ready" by Curtis Mayfield. While this song is not always thought of as "church music," it was perfect for the season of Advent, when the pericopes (standard scripture readings in mainline churches) center on John the Baptist. This song's lyrics parallel the words of John the Baptist in calling for God's people to prepare for God to gather the faithful to the promised land, with faith and repentance being the keys to entering.

Costuming

Costuming will depend on a number of variables, including age of the dancers, type of dance being performed, and budget of the group. Loose fitting clothing, such as stretch pants or warm ups for boys and church dresses for girls are often sufficient. Soft leather shoes or bare feet are adequate when the cost of dancewear is an obstacle for a group. Standard matched dancewear such as leotards, tights, dance shoes (ballet, pointe, jazz), and skirts (pants for boys) are nice when a group has the funds to obtain matching performance uniforms. In churches observant of liturgical seasons, it is sometimes appreciated when dancers can utilize the colors of the season:

Blue or purple	Advent
White	Christmas
Green	Epiphany
Purple	Lent
Black	Good Friday
White	Easter
Red	Pentecost
Green	Sundays after Pentecost
White	Saints' Days and All Saints' Sunday

Use common sense when choosing dance attire. NEVER chose costumes which will distract worshippers from worship. Do not choose costumes which are gaudy or suggestive. Never use low cut or see-through shirts or leotards. There have been times when I needed to alter a costume, which covered less than I had hoped, was too sheer for the temperature, or in some other way made me question whether it would take the focus off the worship. Dancers cannot be outfitted like cabaret dancers or pop singers. The costumes should not steal attention from the dance itself. The purpose of dance is to enrich and edify, not to shock or distract.

It is also important that dancers' movements are not restricted by impossibly confining attire or skirts so large and heavy that inexperienced dancers are apt to trip on them! Costumes should fit all dancers well. Costumes should be chosen to blend with the whole of worship, keeping in mind the specific choreography and dancers' abilities. For example, a dance which utilizes leg and foot movements needs a costume which does not make it difficult to see the legs and feet! Many types of ethnic costumes can be appropriate for specialized or themed dances. Be sure, however, when planning such dances that they are always focussed primarily on the Christian message. If people want to see ethnic dancing, there are many secular places where it is performed. Christian sacred dance, while it can borrow styles from many types of dance, is unique in that it is always a dance which enhances Christian worship and gives glory to God. Dances which have been prepared for performance in a setting other than Christian worship are unlikely to work well as liturgical dance.

In working with artists who design costumes, it is possible to create special costumes which enhance the message of a dance. I have one skirt which was designed to look like tongues of flame when it moved, to remind those watching that sacred Christian dance is a gift of the Holy Spirit.

With very few exceptions, long hair should be pulled neatly back from the face and fastened securely, so it does not become a hindrance.

Unless one is involved with a dance production which includes drama or is in a very large space, make-up is generally not necessary. When dancing for God, it is most appropriate to let the dancers' natural beauty shine through. Dancewear can be purchased easily online through sites like discountdance.com or starstyled.com.

Props

Liturgical dancers often use props. The objects which can be used to enhance liturgical dance are as limitless as the imagination. When bringing any object into the dance, however, practical concerns must first be addressed. As a dance leader, when someone comes to you to ask whether an object they wish to use would be appropriate, first ask questions such as:

1. Will this enhance the worship experience or is it superfluous?
2. Will the weight or size of this object make it difficult to dance or obstruct the view of those watching the dance?
3. If the object is a candle--is this dancer mature and experienced enough to keep this candle from causing damage?
4. If the object involves liquid--is this dancer mature and experienced enough to keep the liquid from spilling while she dances?

Sometimes it is simply best to let the imagination of those watching the dance supply the props. If the dance is part of a drama or in some way conveying a particular story which might suggest sets or props which would be difficult to build and/or work with, it may be best to simply pretend the objects are there. While I do not want liturgical dance to be confused with mime, there are occasions when dance is part of a larger drama or story and mime-like actions might be advocated. This may also happen in dances with particular themes. For example, opening a door or drawing in fishing nets. As a rule, however, dances should not be choreographed with a lot of mime-like movements.

If dance is blended into a larger dramatic production, the props from the dramatic part of the performance may be incorporated into dances done within that production as long as incorporating them does not seem forced or out of place.

Perhaps the most commonly used objects in Christian worship are the elements of bread and wine being brought forward for Eucharist. Processional dances of this sort are common and, as noted above, choreography must be simple enough that spillage is not a concern.

Other objects in a standard Christian sanctuary readily lend themselves to use in liturgical dance as focal points. These include baptismal fonts, paschal candles, processional crosses, and special art, which is unique to a given parish. Sometimes a dance can reflect the art.

For example, at Grace Lutheran Church in Aurora, Illinois, there is a custom-made baptismal font cover with the trinity rendered as three figures dancing on top of the font. I have created dance in which dancers form a circle around the font, reflecting the art (see chapter 8).

Another example is the custom-made advent wreath, about 60 inches in diameter, suspended from the ceiling, at St. Paul Lutheran Church in Sandusky, Ohio. A Christmas dance I choreographed there involved four dancers, who, in the course of the dance, lit the candles on the wreath.

Often ribbons, scarves, or flowers are used in liturgical dance. The size, colors, etc. will depend upon the particular theme, season, and goal of the dance. Large ribbons, like those used in rhythmic gymnastics, can be used when the worship space is extremely large, in order to add color, movement, and visibility. I utilized this particular tool when the University of Illinois Pavilion was turned into worship space for the installation of the first presiding bishop of the newly formed Evangelical Lutheran Church in America in 1987. The red ribbons of the dancers allowed the 5,000 worshippers to more clearly see the processing bishops and dignitaries, led by the dancers. Another item used in the dance on this occasion was pine branches to administer the ancient rite of asperges. The branches were dipped in a very large baptismal font and water was sprinkled on those seated on the main floor, as a remembrance of their common baptism. Asperges is a powerful and tangible reminder of our identity as God's children and common bond as brothers and sisters in Christ. It was wonderful to use dance in bringing this to the worshippers.

Settings for Worship

Worship space can be created almost anywhere. It can be indoors or out, it can be in a small single room or a huge cathedral. When planning a dance, the dancer must always rehearse the dance **in the place where it will be offered** prior to worship. If this is not done, it can lead to unpleasant surprises about space. It is also important to communicate with those organizing the worship about what last minute changes might take place.

When Rev. Charles Maahs was installed as the Bishop of the Missouri-Kansas Synod of the ELCA in 1987, a seminary classmate and I were called upon to dance. We were shown the space and practiced in it. Then, in the final moments before the service was to begin, an entire row of chairs was set up in front of the front pews! This cut significantly into our dance space and made the choreography quite tricky. At one point I leaped and landed so close to a visiting dignitary that, judging by the startled look on his face, I'm sure he thought I was going to end up in his lap. Had the floor been at all slippery, I might have!

Since then I have always asked the person in charge of any large worship service to tell me what potential changes in furniture there might be and I have made clear which spaces must be kept clear if the dance is to proceed as planned. Chairs, flowers, vocal soloists, etc. cannot be inserted at the last minute without telling the dancer! Dancers must be assertive in communicating with worship planners, since people who are unaccustomed to dance in worship never think to ask dancers about their role in the worship and frequently underestimate the space required to execute the choreography. Let me just say that one more time. It's very important: *the dancer must be assertive in communicating his or her needs to the worship planner and even the ushers to be sure the dance space remains clear!*

When worship occurs outdoors, this provides its own distinct challenges and opportunities. If there is no special platform and the dance is performed on the bare earth (whether dirt or grass), bare feet will probably serve better than commercial shoes in terms of both traction and in blending with the natural setting. It will be important to thoroughly examine the space where the dance will be, to know every bump, dip, and inconsistency in the ground's surface. Suggest that the area be cleaned (raked?) prior to the worship, to minimize the possibility of sharp objects or other clutter, which could interfere with the dance. If there are provisions to move the worship indoors in the case inclement weather, be familiar with the alternative worship setting so the dance can be adjusted as necessary.

Sometimes the outdoors can provide a very special experience with dance. A particularly effective dance was performed at the Metro Chicago Synod Professional Leadership Convocation in 1999. A single dancer performed a dance in which she carried large beautiful sections of cloth, suspended by rods that were held in each hand. It gave the impression of wings. As the worshipping community became aware of her presence, she danced amongst a small grove of trees as the sun set behind the treeline, where they could see her from a distance, but she never came close. The pastors who saw this remarked that it was a particularly meaningful experience for them as she, like the Holy Spirit, was something that we sometimes glimpse and watch her work, transfixed by its beauty, yet don't feel like we can ever see it in the proximity we might wish.

Many Christian Churches are designed in a cross shape, with the sides taken up by such things as choir, sacristy, etc, and the primary worship space set up as a long rectangular room with pews on either side of a center aisle, leading up to an east wall altar. This is wonderful for facilitating processional dances, but can pose a challenge for many other types of dance. Learn which pieces of furniture are moveable. Be sure not to dance behind fixed pieces of furniture, such as a lectern, which obstructs the worshippers' view. If there are steps at the front and they are wide enough to be danced upon, it can help the congregation to see better if the dance is performed in that slightly elevated place.

Churches with freestanding center altars and seating on three sides provide an opportunity for creative alternatives in dance, but the choreographer must be constantly aware of what parishioners are seeing from the seats on all three sides to ensure that the view is never completely obstructed for any group of worshippers.

It is important to practice the choreography in the actual worship space where it will be performed. It is often helpful to have a friend sit down in the middle of the pew area and give feedback about what can be easily viewed and what cannot. Dancers are sometimes disappointed to learn that the beautiful footwork, which required so much practice, cannot be seen at all.

The worship space which presented me with the all-time greatest challenge was at the Lutheran School of Theology at Chicago. Our worship space, fondly called "the fish bowl," had seating on a steep incline, which rose up two stories high. I danced down it on a couple of occasions. The first time I did this included some of the most unique choreography of my life. From it I received one of the greatest compliments of my life. One of my professors, Wesley Fuerst, told me it was the most graceful and grace filled thing he had ever seen. The room has since been redesigned.

Warming Up

Anyone with dance background is likely to have his or her own set of preferred warm up exercises. For those who do not, here is a series of very basic stretches to get started. Remember to relax and take deep breaths while performing these stretches. People unaccustomed to exercises or stretches tend to hold their breath, so watch for this. Never bounce.

1. Press chin to chest, hold, then slowly tilt head back as far as it will go and hold. Repeat five times.
2. Look as far as possible to one side, then slowly to the other. Repeat 5 times.
3. Reach arms over head and rise up on toes (feet spread slightly) as far as possible. Repeat 3 times, then, keeping heels firmly on the floor, bend knees as far as possible without letting the heels leave the floor (arms drop to sides). Repeat entire exercise 3 times.

4. Keeping the back flat and legs straight, feet about shoulder width, reach forward (90 degrees), bending at the waist. Stretch and hold 5 seconds. Straighten and place hands on hips, arch back as far as is comfortable. Hold 3 seconds. Reach arm over head and stretch to one side, hold, then the other side. Repeat.
5. Sit down. Roll wrists in circles
6. Do the same with ankles.
7. Put legs straight out in front and stretch forward as far as possible with a flat back. Hold 5-10 seconds. Relax, then repeat.
8. Straddle legs and reach both arms forward with a flat back. Hold 5-10 seconds. Reach to one leg. Hold as before. Reach to the other leg and hold. Repeat whole process twice.
9. Note: this exercise is not for most adult dancers. Lie on your back and bend knees. Place arms at either side of head with hands on the floor, fingertips facing in. Push up as far into a back bend as possible and hold. Return to the floor. Wrap arms around knees and roll back and forth in a ball. Repeat.
10. Deep lunges, slowly, to each side.
11. Jump straight into the air, first with legs together , then with legs shoulder length apart..
12. Extend arms to either side of body. Make small circles with the entire arm. Widen the circles until arms make widest possible circles. Switch direction of circles and repeat.
13. Shake out arms, then legs.

Go dance!!

Chapter 6
Trained and Untrained Dancers

Draping the cross with Chuck Barth for Good Friday at Bethlehem Lutheran Church in Kansas City, Kansas in 1987. Photo by Daniel Borchers

One of the most common uses of liturgical dance is in processionals. Christians have been processing in their worship for as long as there have been grand, formal worship services. This is a place where dance fits in naturally, leading the procession and helping to set the mood for the worship, whether that be somber or joyful. These dances are usually, though not exclusively, simple and repetitive. These often utilize the talents of people in the congregation, young or older, without formal dance training.

Working with untrained dancers

Working with untrained dancers presents a unique set of challenges and opportunities. In my early involvement with liturgical dance, I found such dances very difficult. My own training led me to want big, professional looking pieces and it was difficult to focus on what my willing dancers could do and what would bring the greatest blessing to the worshippers within the context of the worship that had been planned. One of the gifts that came with age and experience was to enjoy working with younger children, who were often the most enthusiastic about offering their gifts of dance within worship.

One drawback to working with untrained dancers is that they do not know the technical language of dance. Movements can easily be described without using dance terms, but it usually takes a little longer. It is simpler to say, "I would like everyone's arms in fifth position," rather than explaining, "I would like everyone's arms up, bent at the elbows to form an unclosed circle, fingers apart, ... " and so on. Given that choreography for untrained dancers is less complicated, the loss of a common language is not as great of a detriment to the process as a dancer might expect. A trained dancer/choreographer who is working with untrained dancers must keep firmly in his or her mind that dance terminology will not be helpful until each term is explicitly explained and demonstrated to the group. It may help, however, to build some common language together as the dance is learned.

It must also be remembered that movements, which may seem simple and ordinary to the choreographer, may seem foreign and difficult to someone who wishes to dance but lacks formal training. The following will seem obvious to non-dancers, but it is worth stating for the sake life-long dancers: it must be remembered that average people, even people who are somewhat athletic, usually CANNOT:

1. do full splits;
2. arrange their feet in fifth position;
3. remember to point their toes at all times;
4. easily do turns of 360 degrees or more;
5. remember a series of dance movements the first time it is given;
6. balance on the toes of one or both feet for long periods of time;
7. stand on one foot and easily lift the back leg to perpendicular or beyond;
8. understand directions in French.

Years of dance training make such things so automatic for dancers that it can cause great frustration that these things do not become automatic for everyone else after a few practice sessions. It took me a number of years to appreciate the fact that non-trained dancers can be wonderful to work with, but will never be able to do the things listed above with the ease of a trained dancer.

Whether the dancers are 5 or 50 years old, a group of untrained dancers gives the leader a certain freedom which may be absent in trained groups. These dancers are not trained to be performers, athletes, or perfectionists. They do not have the egos which sometimes accompany more highly trained dancers who are accustomed to performing and having central roles in a production. There is a sense of equality among a group of untrained people and an understanding that the performance is to God and for God's glory, not to show off the great skill and technical prowess of the dancers themselves.

Working with younger children

In many Christian Churches you will find the largest number of volunteers for liturgical dance from the demographic of five to eight year old girls who are taking dance lessons. Often parents want to see their 3-5 year olds participate in dance at church if there is dance offered in worship. This can be a blessing to a worshipping congregation, but should not be confused with trained dancers as you plan the choreography. Even if a dancer begins lessons at the age of 3, keep in mind that between the ages of three and five, such lessons help with basic coordination, but will not teach much actual dance expertise. It has also been my experience that the attention span of most 3 to 5 year olds does not allow them to keep up with their older counterparts who are studying dance, as you teach choreography to a group. Thus, in most cases, 3-5 year olds should be considered untrained when planning choreography and worked with separately from older counterparts to avoid frustration on the part of everyone involved.

It is imperative that you, as the leader, explain to the group what liturgical dance is and is not. It is not a dance recital. It is not for them to "show off " for parents or grandparents. It is sacred and done to help everyone in the church focus on their worship of God. You may wish to read Scripture with them (see chapter 3) and you should ALWAYS pray with the group before practicing and before offering dances in worship. Pray that God use each member of the group to bring blessings to everyone who sees the dance.

While young children are generally quite limber and flexible, it is still important to warm up as a group before practicing or offering dance in worship. Unlike older, more experienced dancers, this group is probably not able to do individual, unsupervised warm ups, so plan to be very hands-on about this. The last thing anyone needs to deal with is a pulled muscle or other injury. Be thorough.

Warm-ups can also be an excellent vehicle to refocus the group on its purpose. Children are often coming from other activities. They're distracted, running around, and want to visit with friends. After a few minutes of this, the leader needs to bring the group together to focus--as one--on its purpose. You may wish to begin with simple breathing exercises, as this makes extraneous talking more difficult.

Among the blessings of working with this group is that children this age will often offer ideas and opinions about choreography, solicited or unsolicited. Be open. Remember God's Spirit moves within them too! It is sometimes amazing to see how the Spirit moves these young people when they are genuinely focussed on the task at hand and the reason for dancing. I believe there is a special place in God's heart for the innocent exuberance of the young and as a result, the things they say and do can be absolutely inspired.

Sometimes, however, the suggestions are without focus or thoughtfulness. It is your job as the leader to determine what movements will be appropriate in the end. If a child wants to try something she saw a pop singer do on stage, you may need to expand your explanation about what liturgical dance is. Remind them we are dancing for God in church, not for money on MTV, and the style of movement here is reverent, not in any way suggestive.

If an untrained group is comprised of younger children, the greatest limiting factor for your choreography is simply the children's attention span for learning a dance. In this case the dance must be kept very simple and repetitive. Keep in mind that the congregation is an appreciative audience and in the case of very young dancers, they do not expect anything near perfection. The mere presence of such a group helping to lead worship reminds most Christians of Jesus' love for children and admonitions that we enter God's kingdom with childlike faith. The faith, joy, and purity of such liturgical movement is central. As a leader, you must let go of any deep concern for the technical merit of the dance (or lack thereof). Keep the choreography simple and your instructions clear, schedule plenty of short practice times, be patient with your dancers throughout the process, and then let them offer their gift. It is important that the young people feel at ease and accepted. They should have a joyful experience with offering their dance. This will depend in great part on the attitude of the leader.

Teen and adult dancers

The challenge is very different with a group of willing dancers who are teens or adults, who have no formal training in dance. With this group, attention span is not an issue, but unlike the little ones who can't wait to whirl and sway in front of an audience, this group may be somewhat self-conscious. They may worry that they will not be able to perform to everyone's expectations, that their skills are not great enough for the undertaking, or that they simply do not look good in the dance outfit!

Choreographing for a group of adults is very different from working with six year olds and it is important for the leader to be in the right frame of mind at the onset of either endeavor. Prior to hearing the music for the dance, before checking the worship space or meeting for the first time with the dancers, time must be spent in prayer for those dancers (see chapter 5). Learn something about who they are. What are their struggles? What are their joys? It is safe to assume that they are probably somewhat nervous about offering this gift to the worshipping community if they are not accustomed to dancing in public or dancing as worship, as discussed later in this chapter. Pray for them to have strength and patience and courage throughout the process. Pray for them to be blessed as they bring this blessing to others. Then pray for those things for yourself.

If they have volunteered to dance, they obviously have a willingness to offer this particular gift in worship. In theory this seems good to them, yet, getting out there and doing it in public may be harder than they originally thought. Like reading scripture within worship, it is not the act, but the context, which is frightening. People can be great at reading to themselves or reading to their children, but the idea of reading aloud in holy space, the presence of God and their peers, can be daunting. Dance is the same. They may dance in their own kitchen when they're happy, they may dance with their children, they may even dance in public at weddings, but the idea of dancing *for God*, in front of their friends and even strangers, who are all watching *them* . . . . well, that's a different story!

The dance leader can help ease their nervousness. First, explain that this is why time will be spent practicing. Explain that you have not choreographed anything beyond their ability--and be certain you have not. If you find that you have, be willing to modify the choreography. Finally, explain that they are vessels, bringing God's blessing to those around them. It is a holy gift and worth all of their effort in bringing this gift from God to God's people. The vessels are never perfect, only God's gifts are. The vessel's imperfection does not keep the blessing from coming.

This does not mean that prayer and practice are not necessary in preparing a dance. Of course they are! Having done the work to bring the gift of dance into worship, the dancers must then trust God to use them to do just that.

A story from Christian history

You may wish to tell them about an early heresy called **donatism**. Or you may not. If you think your dancers would find this knowledge helpful, here is the story in a nutshell:

In the first through early fourth centuries, Christians were persecuted and many were martyred. Others renounced the faith to escape death. Some of these were church leaders. Some, who followed the teachings of Cyprian, believed that the Church on earth was inextricably linked to the persons who were ordained priests and bishops. There was no Church outside these people. So what happens when one of these priests falters? According to the Donatists, no one could function as a leader if he committed any public sin, which would make him unworthy. Renouncing the faith completely would be absolutely unforgivable and no one who received sacraments from one such as this could trust them to be valid.

Augustine, Bishop of Hippo (North Africa) had to decide what this meant for Christianity. He faced difficult questions. How can the Church exist if the priests renounce their faith and prove themselves unworthy? Could priests or other Christians who had forsaken the Church later return? What of the baptisms these priests had performed? Were they valid if the priest had renounced his faith under duress?

Augustine's answer was yes. God's grace allows us to forgive those who are not strong enough to stand up for their faith. Augustine also affirmed that sacraments performed by such people were still valid, as the sacrament was ultimately from God, not from the priest.

I find this piece of history comforting beyond dance as well. It helps me remember not to confuse God with the imperfect reflection of God we find in the Church. While God is perfect, the Church sometimes stumbles in far greater ways than my feet ever could in a single dance. I must remember that, no matter how far afield a particular Christian, priest, or congregation seems to go, it does not change the power or love of God. THAT can always be trusted. Human frailty does not negate the blessings people receive from imperfect leaders. I often think of this little piece of history and remember to have grace for myself and for those around me, as we falter in a myriad of ways, trying to reflect divine love to one another.

This does not, of course, mean that any dance is appropriate for any worship or that it is any less than vital to practice a dance into its best possible form. I want to be absolutely clear that dancers who lack formal training should not attempt dances which would require formal training! Folk dances and simple dances, such as I have explained in this book, are the best option to allow untrained dancers to offer their gifts in a way which will bless the worshippers. Asking them to attempt movements which are too difficult will only bring frustration to both the dancers and the congregation. But when one's best efforts are made and still there is a mistake, we can take comfort in knowing that this is unlikely to mar the blessings received by those who watch our dance. The dance is more than just our gift, it is God's.

Tripudium

The following is a wonderful ancient step, which can be done with dancers of almost any age. This is one of the oldest recorded dances within Christianity. Doug Adams writes, "The tripudium step was the most common dance step in Christian church processions for a thousand years and fits with any hymns of 2/4, 3/4, or 4/4 time." (Adams p. 20)

In the step, the dancer moves three steps forward, then one step back. This symbolizes our walk with God, in which we move forward with faltering steps-- progressing, yet sometimes failing. It is often danced during Lent. I have done this on Ash Wednesday, letting the dancers lead the congregation toward the imposition of ashes. My favorite hymn to use with this dance is "Ah, Holy Jesus," which can be found in the Lutheran Book of Worship as hymn number 123.

The bare bones simplicity of this footwork makes this dance accessible to all. It is the dance with which I have brought the greatest number of people into actively participating in liturgical dance over the years. Since history only offers us the movement of the feet in this dance, I have added simple arm variations. As this is done with four beats, allowing for the three steps forward and one back, I will explain the arm motions in groups of four commands. The first variation is as follows:

1. fully extended right arm is lifted to 150 degrees (face level) as right foot steps forward
2. left arm is lifted to 150 degrees, parallel to right, as left foot steps forward
3. both arms are lifted higher, to about 165 degrees, as right foot steps forward
4. both arms drop as the dancer takes one step backward

This variation is quite simple and most people can do it. A minor variation on this looks a bit like a really slow windmill. It is as follows:

1. Right arm rises in the front, left in the back to about 45 degrees
2. Each one lifts to just beyond perpendicular
3. Arms cross over head
4. Arms drop again to the dancer's side.

The next variation can be used a couple of different ways. It takes a great deal of balance and control to perform gracefully. If there is a mixed group of dancers, and some have more experience, you may wish to alternate between novice and more experienced dancer in your procession, having the more experienced people try the following:

1. step with right foot

2. step left and pivot toward your back, into a full turn, arms come up for balance
3. complete the turn by stepping out with right foot
4. step back with left foot.

The trick is to make this look effortless. The step back should not look like the dancer is simply catching him/herself. It should be a pronounced, intentional step.

Another way I have utilized dance in Lent, is draping the cross on Good Friday, as pictured on the first page of this chapter. I have danced alone, beginning with the Tripudium, then breaking away into other subdued dancing, then returning to the Tripudium. A second person follows some distance behind, carrying the drape for the cross, never varying from the Tripudium step. When we both reach the cross to be draped, we gently place the drape, reverence the altar and return to our seats. This has been a wonderful way to include people who consider themselves non-dancers.

Chapter 7
Themed Dances

Me with Adrianna Greising, Marika Greising, and Jyotsana Mohan dancing "Come to the Fount of Creation" in 1999.

Within the pericopes of mainline Christian congregations (a three year cycle of Scripture readings), there are many opportunities for dances to illustrate stories from Jesus' life and ministry. There are rich, concrete images of life and discipleship. There are images from everyday life--sweeping, baking, eating, fishing, and images that take us out of the ordinary-- angel choirs singing, baptism in the river, etc. Many of these call out to be shared in the worshipping community with more than just words. This is especially true for the younger members of the congregation, who love to DO rather than only listen.

Two Fishermen

One of my favorite dances, which I originally choreographed for this age group, was danced in 1998 and

1999 at Grace Lutheran Church in Aurora to the music "Two Fishermen." (Copyright 1994 GIA Publications, Inc., Chicago). This dance could certainly be done with dancers of any age or level of experience. Unlike some dances, pointed toes and fluid movement are not a pre-requisite. The motions simply need to be BIG and overstated. When the arms "fling the nets," they fling them as wide as the arms can open, with gestures that are urgent and earnest. This works particularly well with small children because the signal which invites them is actually part of the dance! I have a videotape of this dance with my twin daughters at the age of six. It's inspiring to see their young enthusiasm in these movements, combined with a beautiful reverence for what they are doing, not wanting to miss a cue.

The dance is extremely simple and flexible. It can be done with almost any number of dancers, but a minimum of four is needed and eight is the number I used in the original choreography. By the end of the dance, you may have a large part of the congregation joining you!

Another advantage to this dance is the lack of costuming. The dancers should look like "regular folks" because the dance is about Jesus calling people from everyday life and then those people inviting others to join.

The dance begins with two dancers at the front of the congregation. If this is to be done with the minimum number of dancers (4), a single dancer can begin. I will assume two in the following description, however, as that is ideal.

The dancers face one another. As the music begins, they join hands (on the words "two fishermen"). They swing their arms together toward the congregation (who lived along), back (the Sea of Gali-), and on next measure,

97

with the end of the word, "GaliLEE, they open their arms toward the congregation, as if to throw the nets out.

In the next four measures they pretend to pull the nets back in, using long grasping and pulling motions in the direction of the congregation, one arm at a time. It should look like the nets are big and heavy. It's a long pull from the arm's furthest reach, back to the dancer's body. One leg is out in front (right or left, depending on which side of the dancer is facing the congregation) and weight should shift back and forth from one leg to the other as the nets are pulled in.

With the words, "Now Jesus watched them," they put their right hands flat above their right eyes, as if to look into the distance, then on "from afar," the arm drops. With the words, "then called them each by name," the dancers motion with one arm to the congregation, and may focus specifically on the next dancers who will join them, with a traditional "come on!" motion. It should be big and enthusiastic.

The dancers join hands again as the second set of dancers come running to find their places in the front. On the words, "It changed their lives, these simple men," the original dancers side-chassé (use a galloping motion) away from the congregation, then turn back to face the original direction, toward the congregation. Depending on the space you use for this dance, the direction or distance covered in this movement may need to be adjusted. I had a very wide step we could move onto, which made space for later dancers, so we covered a lot of space on the first verse, then less in subsequent verses. The new dancers joining the dance may need this measure to simply get into their positions. The second and third pairs of dancers may be placed to the left and right of the original ones. If

possible, this original pair may move closer to the altar--
many churches have wide steps leading up to or just inside
the communion rail, then the final pair may come to the
position in which the original two had begun, front, center.

On the words, "They'd never be the same," dancers
take two steps back in the direction from which they came,
each time lifting the knee high. Arms make a slightly open
circle in front of the dancer (first position).

Dancers join hands again and immediately push
back from one another. Then, still holding hands, they pull
the arms above their heads, stepping closer to one another.
This is during the words, "Leave all things you have." The
partners then drop hands, but leave the hands raised, and
pirouette. As the words, "come and follow me" repeat,
each dancer turns her back to the congregation, reaches her
outside hand forward and follows it in a circle, away from
her partner, then back to the original position.

The dance repeats, bringing two more sets of
partners in. The GIA songbook lists four verses for this
song. On the last verse, after the worshippers have seen
the dance repeated 3 times, make clear in your motioning
for people to join that you truly intend that anyone who
wishes to join the dance should come forward. This can be
a wonderful way to lead into a sermon about discipleship.
The mood is set where people are feeling, in a very
immediate way, how difficult it can be to leave one's
comfort zone and step out to answer the call to follow
Jesus!

I found this to be a favorite with young people. The
music is strong and easy to follow. The motions are simple
and tell the story. Children tell the story with a mixture of
joy and reverence that is awe-inspiring. Never

underestimate the power of letting the least among us be our teachers.

Christmas with a Native American touch

This is a simple processional dance that popped into my head one Christmas while I was listening to our church band practice a Native American melody, "Twas in the Moon of Wintertime." I believe it sounds best, as they had done it, with minimal instrumentation. I recommend a single drum and recorder or flute. We did not prepare any costumes. The dancers wore their Christmas dresses. They all chose dresses that facilitated movement. For some of the little girls, this meant it had to be pretty while spinning. I can respect that.

Dancers may process into the space in a single line or from different locations, depending on your sanctuary. When the dancers reach the front of the worship area, they may plan to do this dance across the front, with dancers going to opposite sides, then crossing back, or they may wish to dance up the side aisles. We chose to adapt the dance to the chancel area, once the dancers had all processed in.

To begin the dance, the dancer steps out with the right foot. The right arm is extended straight to the front, left arm to the back, palms down ('twas in). Step left. Gently lower arms a couple inches and bring them back to perpendicular, this time with palms up (the moon), in a pulsing sort of motion. Step right and repeat this arm movement to the other side. Swing arms so that left is in front, right in back, palms down (of winter-). Step, palms up (-time). Full turn forward with arms up (pirouette), then arms come down slowly (when all the birds had fled). This repeats in the next measures (that God the Lord of all the earth sent angel choirs instead). Chassé (tell small children to gallop) right on the words, "before their light," then chassé left to "the stars grew dim."

With the words, "and wandering hunters heard," the dancers hop with one leg extended behind (sauté in arabesque), first on the right foot, then on the left,. Arms are out in front, one higher than the other, then change. On "the hymn," dancers hold, just for a moment, an arabesque position on demi-pointe if possible (balancing on one leg, up on the toe if possible, with the other straight out behind).

With the words, "Jesus, your" the dancers bring the right leg out of the arabesque and step up onto the right toe (pique), bringing the left leg up, bent, with the toe to the knee (retire/ some call this passé). On "king, is born," step backward with the left foot and bend that leg, leaving the right leg straight in front. The weight is on the back leg. Sweep the right hand past the right foot, bending forward at the waist. On the words, "Jesus is born," the dance executes another pirouette (full turn) and finally, with the words, "in excelsis gloria," the body contracts, arms sweep around the sides, palms back, shoulders are down, , then arms rise to over the head and slowly lower. (contraction of the body, arms fifth then second).

This is less complicated than it may seem. It helps to hear the music as you attempt to envision the dance. That melody line and verses of this music are reprinted with the generous permission of GIA publications. To order the full sheet music, please contact GIA at (800) GIA1358.

The mood of this dance is reverent and the movements are slow and careful. It is lovely for setting the mood of a late Christmas Eve worship service.

Come to the Fount . . .

This dance was choreographed for a group of older, trained dancers. The movements are graceful and flowing. It is a dance of inviting and welcoming to God as the "fount of salvation." One might interpret that image to be the water of baptism and wish to use this dance at a baptism or confirmation/affirmation of baptism. At Grace Lutheran, part of this was danced around the baptismal font. It may be hard to see in the picture at the opening of chapter 7, but the font at Grace, pictured there, had a sculpture of a dancing trinity on its lid, which made this even more visually interesting. The tune is a traditional Irish piece, which will very likely be familiar. The words are adapted by John Ylvisaker and can be found in his book, *Borning Cry*.

The dance begins with four dancers, two on each end of the chancel area (assuming it's not more than about 12 feet across), one in front of another, facing the congregation. We had a step, allowing the dancers furthest away from the congregation to better be seen, which was nice. In the opening movements, all dancers move to their right, then left. It begins with a sauté, tombé, pas de bourée to each side. That is, dancers give a little hop to the right, landing on the right foot, then step behind with the left, switch weight to left then back to right, then hop to the left and repeat. As this is done, the words "There's a land that is fairer than . . . " are sung. Arms extend out to each side. On the word, "sunshine," all dancers do a chaîné turn toward the center. That's a full turn with legs about shoulder width apart. Arms come straight up, also about shoulder width.

With the words, "There's a land that is finer," the dancers repeat the sauté, tombé, pas de bourée, right and left (be sure you have left enough space between you to do this) and do the chaîné turn back to their starting places on the words, "than gold."

In the next measure, with the words, "There's a world where we love," the dancers chassé leading with the right leg, then left, moving toward the center (if it's a small chancel, they may move past one another). On the words, "for a lifetime" the dancers lunge away from the center and circle the inside arm, starting with the arm down, around in front, full circle, and back down. The outside arm is still, at about a 45 degree angle from the body, out to the side.

Next, with the words, "There's a world where we'll never grow old," dancers gracefully walk to their places around the font (or predetermined place, in a circle, in front of the altar).

As the music comes to the refrain, "So come to the fount," each dancer, individually, on each beat, lifts her right arm, with a signal of beckoning (see picture at the start of chapter 7). With the words "of creation," the dancers weave their hands into a circle. Each arm comes up, so it is visible to those watching, then comes down and grasps the hand of the dancer beside her, first left, then right crossing over it.

The dancers move slowly, clockwise, in a circle, with hands clasped, as the congregation, choir or other vocalist(s) sings, "where the water of life is flowing . . . ." On the word free, the hands release, rise up from the center of the circle, each dancer's arms moving up past her head, at shoulder width apart, than circle down past her sides. The dancers arch back slightly.

As the vocalist(s) sing, "Come and drink from the wells," the dancers arms weave together once more, left, then right crossing over, and dancers once more move clockwise around the circle, to the words, "of salvation."

Now the dancers raise their arms up, still clasped together, and turn their bodies to allow the arms to uncross. They will end up facing out rather than into the circle. As this is done, the dancers continue to move in the clockwise circle. The words of the refrain are, "where the Saviour is waiting for."

On the word, "thee," dancers step out of the circle and take places again, two in front, two in back, either at the center of the chancel or at the sides where they began the first verse. If it takes more than this one measure for your dancers to accomplish this, you may wish to have the musicians pause or play a couple extra notes before beginning the next verse.

If your dancers are at the center, the next verse is just like the first, except that the dancers begin in the center, move out and back, rather than starting at the sides, moving in and then out. If they return to their starting positions from the first verse, the dance repeats in the second verse, exactly as it was in the first. It works either way.

For costuming we used black leotards, black tights, black skirts, and a green sash. We did not happen to use this for a baptism or other special occasion, it was just another "green" Sunday after Pentecost. We used to joke that there must have been about a hundred "Sundays after Pentecost." In reality, there are twenty seven or so.

This dance sounds far more complicated than it really is, though the turning as the arms unwind takes a little practice. If arms aren't all crossed properly, it may not work. It needs to be practiced until all the movements look calm and fluid. The tone it sets is one of peace and tranquility.

688 Two Fishermen

1. Two fish-er-men, who lived a-long The Sea of Gal-i-
2. And as he walked a-long the shore 'Twas James and John he'd
3. O Si-mon Pe-ter, An-drew, James And John be-lov-ed
4. And you, good Chris-tians, one and all Who'd fol-low Je-sus'

lee, Stood by the shore to cast their nets In-
find, And these two sons of Zeb-e-dee Would
one, You heard Christ's call to speak good news Re-
way, Come leave be-hind what keeps you bound To

to an age-less sea. Now Je-sus watched them
leave their boats be-hind. Their work and all they
vealed to God's own Son. Su-san-na, Mar-y,
trap-pings of our day, And lis-ten as he

from a-far Then called them each by name; It
held so dear They left be-side their nets. Their
Mag-da-lene Who trav-eled with your Lord, You
calls your name To come and fol-low near, For

changed their lives, these sim-ple men; They'd nev-er be the same.
names they'd heard as Je-sus called; They came with-out re-gret.
min-is-tered to him with joy For he is God a-dored.
still he speaks in var-ied ways To those his call will hear.

Leave all things you have And come and fol-low

me, And come and fol-low me.

Text: Suzanne Toolan, SM, b.1927. © 1986, GIA Publications, Inc.
Tune: LEAVE ALL THINGS, CMD with refrain; Suzanne Toolan, SM, b.1927. © 1970, GIA Publications, Inc.

361 'Twas in the Moon of Wintertime

1. 'Twas in the moon of win-ter-time, When all the birds had
2. The ear-liest moon of win-ter-time Is not so round and
3. Oh, chil-dren of the for-est free, The an-gel song is

fled, That God the Lord of all the earth Sent
fair As was the ring of glo - ry 'round The
true; The ho - ly child of earth and sky Is

an - gel choirs in - stead; Be - fore their light the
help - less in - fant there. The chiefs from far be -
born this day for you; Come kneel be - fore the

stars grew dim, And wan-d'ring hunt-ers heard the hymn:
fore him knelt With gifts of fox and bea - ver pelt.
ra - diant boy, Who brings you beau - ty, peace, and joy.

Je - sus your king is born; Je - sus is born, in ex -

cel - sis glo - ri - a.

Text: Jean de Brebeuf, 1593-1649; trans. by Jesse E. Middleton, 1872-1960. © 1927. Frederick Harris Music Co. Ltd.
Tune: UNE JEUNE PUCELLE, 8 6 8 6 88 with refrain; French melody; arr. by Marty Haugen, b.1950, © 1992. GIA Publications, Inc.

Used by permission. Copyright 1992, GIA Publications, Inc. (800) GIA-1358

Come To The Fount Of Creation

C modal

There's a land that is fair - er than sun - shine; there's a land that is fin - er than gold. There's a world where we love for a life - time; there's a world where we'll nev - er grow old. So come to the fount of cre - a -___ tion, where the wa - ter of life is flow-ing free. ____ Come and drink from the wells of sal - va - tion where the Sav - ior is wait - ing for thee. Here the

Text: John Ylvisaker © 1991 John C. Ylvisaker
Music: "Sally Gardens", trad. Irish, arr. J.Y. © 1991 John C. Ylvisaker

Used by permission. Copyright 1991. John Ylvisaker, P.O. Box 321,
Waverly, Iowa 50677. (319) 352-4396.

Chapter 8
Special Events

Dancing at my wedding to David E. Mertz on October 12, 2003 at Lutheran Church of the Good Shepherd in North Aurora, IL. The young man to the left is my son, Alex. The presiding pastor is Rev. Katherine North. Photo by Elizabeth Wuerffel.

Dance is often requested for special occasions like baptisms, confirmations, weddings, or even funerals, as described in the first chapter. It may be that the confirmand, bride, groom, or deceased has been involved with dance or performing arts, and dance is requested in his or her honor, or perhaps the worship planner simply feels that dance will enhance the mood of the occasion. Dance is also likely to be requested for major Church festivals like Christmas and Easter when it is a part of a congregation's regular worship. In this chapter I will give some choreography and some ideas around which to build choreography for events such as these. Chapter 7 includes a Christmas dance, which I chose to include with processionals rather than special events, as well as a dance which would fit well at a baptism.

Easter

One of the most joyful dances I did with the dancers at Grace Lutheran was to the traditional song "Since I Laid My Burden Down." It's an old traditional song, probably familiar to most people. This song was reworked by John Ylvisaker, based on 2 Timothy 2, in his song "A Joy That Has No End," which is reprinted by permission at the end of this chapter. This song appeared under the title "Glory, Glory, Hallelujah" in the *Borning Cry* songbook.

This dance could be used for Easter, a baptism, or any joyful celebration. This dance worked particularly well in the particular worship setting we had there, with pews on three sides of the altar area. A dancer was stationed on each side of this area, in front of a group of pews. We had two dancers facing one another in the front, since they were small and their steps covered less space.

Though in the sheet music the song begins with the verse, we chose to begin with the refrain: "Glory, glory, hallelujah."

One arm is thrown decisively into the air at about a 45 degree angle from the head on each side with each "glory." The arms sweep down in a circle in front of the body and return to that place on the word, "hallelujah." With the next line, the dancer reaches front with the right arm , turns 360 degrees, bringing the other arm into a circle in front of the body (first position). She then immediately adds another 180 degree turn, while bending the arms in, with hands pointing in toward the shoulders, then extending past the head, in a movement of setting something down. The words are "When I laid my burden down." These words and motions repeat. This is the song's refrain.

For the verse, dancers gallop (chassé) once then skip once on the right and then left (sauté). The dancer stops and with both feet square (in parallel) on the floor and throws each arm into a perpendicular position to each side. The words in the first verse at this point are "died for us." So the arms remind us of the cross. The next words are "and rose again." Here the dancers' arms swing in as they squat down, then the dancer pops up in the air, landing on one foot with arms raised over head. The kids enjoyed that part.

Next the dancer brings his or her leg up, bent, turns 180 degrees (en dedans pique turn), then extends the leg forward (developpé front). After a couple quick (running) steps, the dancer leaps (grand jeté), lands and turns back to face the direction from which he or she came. The last movement of the dance is a little hard to describe because it is from Indian dance. The parents of some of my dancers were from India and the oldest girl of the group often offered suggestions for choreography. I loved to watch them do Indian dances--they were absolutely lovely. Still, this does not help me with a name for this movement she added to this dance, but I'll do my best to describe it: in demi plié (knees slightly bent) the dancer brings her hands nearly together on one side, at about ear level, circles her hands completely around at the wrist (while holding the arms in the same slightly bent position to one side) and then bends both knees and arms deeper on the last note.

Then comes the refrain and next verse. We did a number of verses of this and it was quite an aerobic workout! The dance brought big smiles from both the dancers and the people watching (especially parents). They could see how the kids had helped to create this.

Funeral

In chapter one I described a dance from the funeral of a young teacher in Brookfield, Illinois. For reasons stated in that chapter, it will be nearly impossible for me to give you the full choreography for this. It was not videotaped. I can, however, outline the dance.

In the first verse of "Now the Green Blade Rises," (Lutheran Book of Worship hymn #148) a single dancer, symbolizing the life of the deceased, dances forward. The dance should be consistent with who this person was. Since the teacher for whom I was dancing, was also classically trained, the dance I did was based solidly in ballet. In describing this particular dance, I will refer to this dancer as "she," though it could certainly be a man.

During the second verse, which talks about Christ, the dancer moves toward the Pascal Candle, which is always a symbol for Christ's presence in the worship space. She lights a small candle, which she may have brought with her as she danced forward or may be placed near the Paschal Candle for her to pick up. After lighting her candle off the Paschal or "Christ" Candle, she moves to the center front of the worship space, holding the candle.

While the dancer has been lighting the candle, some of her students have begun to walk forward slowly. If this is not for a teacher, then children, friends, or colleagues may dance this role. They meet her at the front at the end of the second verse.

During the third verse, she lights each of their candles off hers, symbolizing the light she has passed on through her life and/or teaching. It is the light of knowledge, the light of friendship, the light of hope, the light of joy in living. It is a light which, ultimately, comes from God, as we saw by it's source in the Paschal Candle. As each student candle is lit, that person walks to a different place in the worship space, holding the lit candle. This reminds us how the things we pass on to others go with them when we part ways.

At the end of the third verse, there is a somber pause. A bell tolls in the distance. This can be a church bell, a tone from a setting on the organ or synthesizer, or any other instrument which could produce such as sound. It needs to ring slow, sad, and hollow. As it rings, the students/friends stop wherever they are standing and look back to the single dancer. That dancer blows out her candle and bows her head, symbolizing the death. I have done this dance on two occasions and both times I could hear, or was later told, of the muffled gasps and choked tears at this point. It is a powerful moment and I believe it helps in the grieving process for the mourners to see concrete representation of what they are feeling. Don't rush this part. Let the bell toll a number of times before starting the next verse.

As the final verse begins ("When our hearts are wintry, grieving, or in pain") the dancer begins to walk slowly down the main aisle toward the door. But as she does, she looks up, individually, at each of the other dancers where they stand. ("Your touch can call us back to life again") . A few steps should be taken between each. As she does this, each one gracefully acknowledges her with a wave of an arm, a solemn nod of a head, or a repositioning of the body. They acknowledge that they understand how they take a part of her with them as they continue through their lives ("Fields of our hearts that dead and bare have been; love is come again like wheat arising green."). Finally, the dancer quietly exits through the back. The other dancers walk solemnly, candles still lit, to the nearest exit. The extreme mood of reverence of mourning here demand that all dancers are absolutely silent as they exit. There can be no talking or extraneous sound. It is probably unnecessary to mention this, unless the students involved happen to be younger.

Wedding

At the wedding pictured above, the processional music was Mozart's Divertimenti No. 7, 1st Menuetto. The junior bridesmaids processed in dancing. The bridesmaids walked as the music shifted, then at the end of the piece, as the music returned to the refrain from the beginning, the bride danced forward. It set the tone of joyful celebration for the rest of the event.

Signing

Sign language can be a wonderful complement to dance. I have seen songs and dances where children were taught signing and it was very moving. I highly recommend adding dance as well! Children love to learn both songs and dances with sign language. They will, of course, need to be taught by someone with training in this area. Children love the fact that it is an actual language that some people understand and use. The strength of signing is that it is a very expressive language and brings out emotion in a way that words often cannot. It is the perfect complement to dance as both communicate on a level that allows for deep expression and embodied ideas. Using a few signed words within the dance, not trying to sign too many of the words, works best. Children love to sign on refrains of songs.

The only time I have used American Sign Language in a dance, was in 1995, when I was working on learning this language. I found some video of this dance, as I was looking for other dances in my mountains of 8mm tapes. It was a combination of dance and signing, interwoven. I might have tried to include it, but the lighting was so bad on the video that I could barely see parts of the dance and don't remember enough of it to reproduce it without the help of that tape.

Simple congregational movements

Often I have helped groups of dancers, or simply young people, lead a congregation in simple movements which fit with a song (see picture at beginning of chapter 3). This can be considered a form of dance ministry. The movements usually reflect the words quite literally. It takes no formal training whatsoever to create such dances to give new life to a congregation's favorite songs. This can be something a congregation enjoys a great deal. Young people often learn songs with such movements at youth gatherings and bring them home to their congregations.

A wide variety

There are a wide variety of dance forms and ways in which dance can be used in worship. Worship may begin with a processional dance. Dance can be used to set the mood for the worship experience as a whole or to prepare for a particular part of the worship, such as eucharist or imposition of ashes. It might be as simple as arm motions from the worshippers in the pews or as complicated as a highly trained group presenting the core message or "sermon." It can be part of a drama. It can have an ethnic flavor, a folk dance feel, or involve pointe shoes. If there is some aspect of dance or style of dance about which you desire further information, the International Sacred Dance Guild can be a wonderful resource. The Guild can help connect you to other dancers, worship opportunities, workshops, and festivals.

Go to www.sacreddanceguild.org. or write to Sacred Dance Guild, P.O. Box 187, Temple, N.H. 03084. The Guild welcomes dancers of all religions, celebrating the universality of dance as a means of interacting with the divine.

God's Spirit moves God's people in countless ways. Let those who are moved to dance, praise God in the dance!

A Joy That Has No End

So, re - mem - ber / our de - fend - er / died for
For in Christ is / all our sor - row, / and in
For in Christ we / find sal - va - tion, / and in

Refrain: Glo - ry, glo - ry, / hal - le - lu - jah! / since I

us and / rose a - gain, / that he is our
Christ our / end - less joy, / and in Christ hope
Christ our / full re - lease, / and in Christ our

laid my / bur - den down. / Glo - ry, glo - ry,

lov - ing Sav - ior, / and a joy that / has no end.
for to - mor - row, / that no - bod - y / can de - stroy.
great re - demp - tion, / and in Christ our / last - ing peace.

hal - le - lu - jah! / since I laid my / bur - den down.

From II Timothy 2; J.Y. © 1989 John C. Ylvisaker; Music: "Since I Laid My Burden Down", trad. American

Bibliography

Adams, Doug. Congregational Dancing in Christian Worship. The Sharing Company, 1976.

Daniels, Marilyn. The Dance in Christianity, A History of Religious Dance Through the Ages. Ramsey, New Jersey: Paulist Press, 1981.

Davies, J.G. Liturgical Dance: An Historical, Theological and Practical Handbook. London, SCM Press, 1984

Deiss, Lucien and Gloria Gabriel Weyman. Dancing For God. Cincinatti, Ohio: World Library of Sacred Music, 1965.

Deitering, Carolyn. The Liturgy as Dancing and the Liturgical Dancer.

Eliot, T.S. Four Quartets. New York: Harcourt, Brace & World, Inc., 1943

Fisher, Constance. Dancing With the Early Christians. Austin: The Sharing Company, 1983.

Gage, Ronald, with Thomas Kane and Robert VerEecke. Introducing Dance in Christian Worship. Washington, D.C.: The Pastoral Press, 1984.

Greely, Andrew. "Empirical Liturgy: The Search for Grace." New York: America Press, Inc., 1987.

The Holy Bible. New Revised Standard Version.

Nelson, James B. Embodiment, An Approach to Sexuality and Christian Theology. Minneapolis: Augsburg Publishing House, 1979.

Reese, W.L. Dictionary of Philosophy and Religion. Eastern and Western Thought. New Jersey: Humanities Press, 1980.

Rochelle, Jay C. "The Contemplative Ground for Craft."

Rock, Judish, and Normal Mealy. Performer as Priest & Prophet. San Francisco: Harper & Row, 1988.

Sorell, Walter. The Dance Through the Ages. New York: Grosset & Dunlap, 1967.

Stewart, Iris J. Sacred Woman, Sacred Dance. Rochester, Vermont: Inner Traditions, 2000.

Walker, Williston with Richard A. Norris, David W. Lotz, and Robert T. Handy. A History of the Christian Church. Fourth Edition. New York: Charles Scribner's Sons, 1985.

Music Resources

Gather Comprehensive. Chicago: GIA Publications, Inc., 1996. To order music, call (800) GIA-1358, www.giamusic.com

Lutheran Book of Worship. Minneapolis: Augsburg Publishing House, 1992 (eleventh printing).

Ylvisaker, John. Borning Cry, Worship for a New Generation. New Generation Publishing, 1992., www.ylvisaker.com

Ordering Information

For copies of this book, send $12 plus $3 shipping/handling to:

Liturgical Dance Book
P.O. Box 119
North Aurora, Illinois 60542

Add $.50 postage for each additional book. For larger orders (over 5 books), ask about postage discounts (address above). Questions may also be directed through e-mail to deenabess@yahoo.com

Residents of Illinois, add 7.5% sales tax

About the cover:
In October of 1987 I did the choreography for a processional dance for the Constituting Convention of the Evangelical Lutheran Church in America. I danced it with the Rev. Irma Seaton Wolf. The day of the convention, I realized that all my friends and colleagues were directly participating in the event and I had no one to take a picture of the dance! I never got a single picture. After I flew home to Kansas, I asked my husband to at least get a picture of me in the outfit that had been specially designed for this event, with a skirt that was meant to look like tongues of flame to symbolize God's Holy Spirit. This is the picture you see on the cover.

A Request
If anyone out there has pictures of the dance from this event, I would be grateful to see them!
(deenabess@yahoo.com)

Photo by Steve M. Kapas
Creative Photography

About The Author

Deena Bess Sherman was born in the great state of New York. She earned her B.A. from Valparaiso University and M.A. from the Lutheran School of Theology at Chicago. She has published curricula for adult and teen Christian education through Augsburg Fortress Press and Group Publishing. She returned for a time to teach theology at her alma mater, Valparaiso University. She has danced in churches from Wilmington, Delaware to Cheyenne, Wyoming. She currently resides with her husband and three children near Chicago.